Sultan Mehmed

The Conqueror

Mariam Seddiq

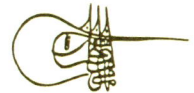

Copyright © 2023 by Mariam Seddiq

All rights reserved.

No part of this book may be reproduced in any form or by any electronic or mechanical means, including information storage and retrieval systems, without written permission from the author, except for the use of brief quotations in a book review.

ISBN:

9780645485417 EPUB

9780645485400 Perfect Bound

Map of Ottoman Expansion by T.R. Saldin, Al Qasim Publishers, trs.ridhwan@gmail.com

PICTURE CREDITS

All pictures by Mariam Seddiq except for:

Topkapı Palace Museum: 20, 81, 88; Fort Nelson, public domain: 53; Gallica Digital Library, public domain, 58; *Liber insularum Archipelagi*, Universitäts- und Landesbibliothek, Düsseldorf, public domain: 74, 75; Istanbul Metropolitan Municipality, 134.

Say, "Indeed, my prayer, my rites of sacrifice, my living and my dying are for Allāh, Lord of the worlds.
(The Qur'an, Al-'An'am, 162 - 163)

Contents

1. OSMAN'S DREAM — 1
   "To destroy a people, you must first sever their roots." Aleksandr Solzhenitsyn

2. MEHMED'S EARLY LIFE — 21
   "Your father has sent me to instruct you, but also chastise you, in case you should not obey me." Mullah Gurani

3. A YOUNG SULTAN — 31
   "(Mehmed) forged his bold plans ... with youthful impetuosity and daring, a sharp and penetrating judgement uncommon for his age ... he was far superior ... in military talent and political insight and skill." Franz Babinger

4. THE CONQUEST OF CONSTANTINOPLE — 45
   "Verily you shall conquer Constantinople. What a wonderful leader will her leader be, and what a wonderful army will that army be!" Prophet Muhammad

5. BUILDING ISTANBUL — 69
   "The Seat of the Roman Empire is Constantinople and he who is and remains Emperor of the Romans is also the Emperor of the whole earth." George Trapezunitios, Greek Scholar, 15th century

6. OTHER CONQUESTS — 87
   "If the hair of my beard knew my plans, I would pull it out and burn it." Sultan Mehmed II

Serbia	90
Aegean Islands	90
On the way to Hungary	93
Greece	98
The Pope's call for a Crusade	100
Trebizond	102
Wallachia and Dracul	105
Lesbos	108
Bosnia	110
Albania and war with Venice	113
Negroponte	116
War with Venice	119
Karaman and Eastern Enemies	121
Death of Çelebi Mustafa	125
Black Sea	126

Peace with Venice	128
The Knights of Rhodes	130
Italy	132

7. MEHMED'S LEGACY — 135
The Great Eagle is dead! La grande aquila è morta!

Sultans of the Ottoman Empire	151
Bibliography	153
Index	155

Chapter 1

OSMAN'S DREAM

"To destroy a people, you must first sever their roots." Aleksandr Solzhenitsyn

History intrigues us and forces us to reflect. As 20th century philosopher and historian Aleksandr Solzhenitsyn said, without our history we lose our very existence. Our past is significantly intertwined with our present and future. It opens the door to who we were, who we are, and where we are heading.

It is difficult to imagine a twenty-one-year-old toppling a thousand-year-old empire and gaining the title of one of the greatest leaders. But Mehmed II rose from the shadows of giants to make and change history. He became the seventh sultan of the Ottoman Empire and gained many extraordinary titles, the most popular of all being the Conqueror, *Al-Fatih* in Arabic, or *Ebu'l-Feth*, the Father of Conquest. He was also known as the Grand Turk, the 'Lord of Two Lands' - Rumelia and Anatolia - 'and of the Two Seas' - the Mediterranean and the Black Sea. With obvious hesitation the Byzantines acknowledged his claim to the title of Caesar of the Roman Empire, *Kayseri Rum* in Arabic. When he died unexpectedly at the age of 49, his enemies rejoiced and chanted that the 'Great Eagle' had died, *La grande aquila è morta!*

Mehmed's story began nine-hundred years before his birth. His ancestors escaped the snow-clad Altai mountains of Central Asia, located in the modern borders of Russia, Kazakhstan, East Turkestan, now the Xinjiang province of China and Mongolia. These mountains covered 845,000 square km, stretched 2000 km and rose to heights of 4.5 km, creating a rugged landscaped with majestic views, humbling Mehmed's ancestors but also helping them to become fierce warriors in the pursuit of survival. In these striking mountains his ancestors found iron and they became experts in metal work and gained the name *Turk,* which is translated as 'helmet'. During the 6th century, groups of these nomadic Turkic tribes merged to defend themselves against invading armies.

The eastern Central Asian Turks were known as Oğuz, and were forced to escape these pristine mountains and journey across the Middle East in search of a home. During the 7-10th centuries the Oğuz Turks travelled through modern Iran and into Iraq. There, the Abbasid caliphate (the ruling Islamic empire between 750-1258 CE, from its capital Baghdad) noticed the discipline of the Oğuz warriors and the expertise of their mounted archers. These Oğuz warriors' fame had spread as far as Morocco and Spain and some were even employed in the Eastern Roman Empire's army. The Abbasid caliphate appreciated their horsemanship and recruited them into the caliphate's army. Some Oğuz warriors converted to Islam through serving in the caliphate army or through their dealings with Muslim merchants. A bond was formed with Islam shaping the course of Turkic history.

Mehmed's life was heavily influenced by his connection to Islam. In the early 7th century, Islam emerged as an ideological and political revelation in the Arabian Peninsula. It delivered a simple message that there was only One God and that Muhammad was His final Prophet and Messenger. People from all ranks of Arabian society accepted this message, particularly the oppressed. They rejected all other deities, including the hundreds of idols that were the gods worshipped in Arabia. Islam called people to worship the One

Creator of the universe and to abide by and establish His commandments. These commandments were very much linked to the Judeo-Christian Biblical message, which Islam came to re-establish and amend. The Prophet Muhammad received the words of God in the form of the Qur'an. Muslims relied on the Qur'an as their prime source of law but also viewed the Prophet's explanations of the Qur'an and his life as the second source of law; this was known as his Sunnah and was recorded in literature known as hadith.

When Islam first emerged in the city of Makkah in 610 CE, it faced fierce opposition from Arabia's ruling elite who wished to maintain the status quo. For the first thirteen years of the Prophet Muhammad's message, Muslims faced persecution and death, causing the Muslims to escape and find refuge elsewhere.

In a city called Yathrib, approximately 400 km north of Makkah, the tribal leaders learned about Islam's message and asked the Prophet to come and seek refuge with them. They saw Islam as a means to end the tribal conflict that existed in their city. Upon the Prophet's migration, this city became known as *Al-Madinah al-Munawwarah* (The Luminous City) or *Madinat Rasul Allah* (City of the Messenger of God) and became the very first Islamic state. On many occasions the ruling elite of Makkah sent large-scale armies to Madinah to kill the Prophet Muhammad and end Islam's message. These were the Battle of Badr (624 CE); the Battle of Uhud (625 CE) and the Battle of the Trench (627 CE) where Madinah was besieged for nearly a month. Amid all this conflict and struggle for survival, the Prophet gave his followers glad tidings of future victories.

A remarkable hadith of Prophet Muhammad intrigued the Muslim community for centuries after his death. In the barren desert of Arabia, where the young Muslim community only numbered a few thousand and faced a constant threat of attack from its enemies, the Prophet prophesied that one day a great Muslim leader and his great army would conquer Constantinople. Constantinople was the capital of the Eastern Roman Empire, also referred to as the Byzantine Empire. The Prophet promised his followers that they would not only overcome immediate threats, but they would conquer and end a reigning superpower. It was a promise that reached for the stars, and it gave the young Muslim community a thirst for the impossible. Eight hundred years later, Muslims believed that Mehmed II embodied and realised this prophecy.

After the death of the Prophet in 632 CE, Islamic territory spread at an amazing speed. Within one hundred years, the caliphate had spread across three continents, into Asia, North Africa and parts of Europe. The caliphate is the Islamic system of government, and its leader is known as the caliph, which means the successor or caretaker of the Prophet. Also spelt as khaleefah, his role was to apply the Islamic law, *sharia*, and manage the needs of the people. The term khaleefah was also used for the general Muslim community as the human being is regarded as a representative of God on earth, to worship God and establish His commandments.

It was a religious obligation upon the Muslims to appoint a caliph (khaleefah) and pledge their allegiance to him, and it was not to be hereditary or influenced by nepotism. The Qur'an explains the duties of a khaleefah:

> *"Verily! We have placed you as a successor (khaleefah) on earth, so judge you between men in truth (and justice) and follow not your desires – for it will mislead you from the Path of Allah." (The Qur'an, Sad, 26)*

The first four caliphs after the Prophet Muhammad were regarded as the 'Rightly Guided Caliphs' (*Al-Khulafa Ar-Rashidun*) because they followed strictly in the footsteps of the Prophet. They were Abu Bakr As-Seddiq (r.632–634); 'Umar bin al-Khattab (r.634-644); 'Uthman bin 'Affan (r.644–656) and Ali ibn Abi-Talib (r.656-661). They were also known as *Amir Al-Mu'mineen* (the Leaders of the Believers). Later, the caliphate became more of a dynasty ruled by families such as the Umayyads (r.661–750) and then the Abbasids (r.750-1258).

The early caliphate faced two serious ancient superpowers: the Persian Empire and the Eastern Roman Empire. Undeterred, the Muslims managed to defeat the Persian army in the Battle of Qadisiya in 636 CE and toppled the entire Persian Empire by 651 CE. They successfully pushed back the Eastern Roman Empire to the outskirts of modern-day Middle East after the famous Battle of Yarmouk in 636 CE which enabled the Muslims to capture Palestine and Syria. By 642 CE, Egypt had also come under Muslim control. These lands were important sources of wealth and status and their loss was devastating for the Eastern Roman Empire. This clash between the Muslims and the Romans continued for another 800 years.

The Eastern Roman Empire was founded by Constantine the Great, who had moved the Roman capital from Italy to Byzantium in 330 CE calling it *Nova Roma*, New Rome. This city was later named Constantinople, after its founder, Constantine. By the 5th century, while the city of Rome – once the heart of the Roman Empire – fell to barbarian invaders, the Eastern Roman Empire and its capital Constantinople grew in prestige and glory. Historically the Roman Empire did not fall during the 5th century, only its western half ceased to exist. While the Eastern Roman Empire did develop a distinct history of its own, it continued to be known as the Roman Empire. In the mid-16th century, a German writer first used the label Byzantine to refer to the Eastern Roman Empire. The name Byzantine was derived from Greek, *Byzas*, the name of the first Greek settler in Constantinople. And only from the mid-19th century, the reference to Roman Empire as Byzantine Empire or Byzantium became the norm. This change delegitimised the Roman heritage of Constantinople and favoured the western European states as the 'true' successors of the Roman empire.

For a thousand years, Constantinople was Byzantine's symbol of power. It kept its Roman law and political institutions, but it favoured

Greek culture and language. During the reign of Emperor Justinian (r. 527–65 CE), the Byzantine Empire was at an impressive height as it spread across the Mediterranean, Italy, the Balkans, Anatolia, and the Middle East. By the 7th century, however, much of Byzantine territory in the Middle East had been taken by the Muslims and by the 11th century, its Anatolian territory had been taken by the Seljuk Turks.

From the time the Prophet Muhammad prophesied the conquest of Constantinople, there was a zealous drive by the Muslims to conquer this Roman treasure. From the 7th century onwards, there were seven Muslim attempts to besiege Constantinople, but to no avail.

The first naval attack was initiated by the close companion of the Prophet, Caliph 'Uthman bin 'Affan in 653 CE. This battle took place in the Mediterranean Sea and was called the Battle of the Mast (in Arabic, *Dhat al-Sawari*) because the Byzantine navy raised crosses on their ships' masts. While the Muslim naval fleet was outnumbered, two hundred to the Byzantine five hundred, the battle proved victorious for the Muslims. The Muslims tactically tied their ships together to create a single unit and threw chains at the Byzantine ships to haul them in. This battle made the Byzantine Emperor, Constans II, turn back to Constantinople in defeat. While it did not yet lead to the conquest of Constantinople, it made the Muslims grow in confidence and continue their expansion across North Africa and into Cyprus and the Mediterranean Sea. It was really the start of subsequent campaigns to overthrow the Eastern Roman Empire.

The second attempt to conquer Constantinople took place in 664 CE, led by the first Umayyad Caliph, Mua'wiya ibn Abi Sufyan. The Anatolian winter was the first obstacle that the Muslim army faced. It prevented them from reaching and besieging the city. However, the Muslims remained persistent, and four years later in 669 CE, a third attempt was organised with a larger navy that crossed the Dardanelles: the passage of water connecting the Mediterranean Sea to the Bosphorus. Historians differ on the actual year that this first Arab siege took place: some claim it was 672 CE or earlier. It was the first siege of Constantinople during the Umayyad Caliphate.

The Muslims tried every resource that they had but the city's walls remained invincible. They besieged the city for seven years and during the dreadful Anatolian winter they would retreat to a nearby island called Cyzicus and return in the summer months. It was during this time that the great companion of Prophet Muhammad died. He was Abu Ayyub al-Ansari, in whose house the Prophet had resided until his own place was built in Madinah. Abu Ayyub was nearly eighty years old when he joined the battle, his age did not deter him. He had fallen ill during the siege and had instructed the Muslim general to persevere in breaching the walls of Constantinople and to bury him there. Today, in Istanbul, an entire suburb and mosque are named in honour of Abu Ayyub, an area believed to be his burial site.

After seven years, the Muslim troops were exhausted. They could not match the Byzantine use of Greek fire; a flame used for the first time that combusted with water and burn down whatever it touched. By 678 CE, the Muslims realised the futility of their efforts and retreated. Although it was a crushing defeat, the tenacity of the Muslims to cross Byzantine territory with approximately 80,000 soldiers and try to end Byzantine reign hadn't gone unnoticed by the Romans. A forty-year peace deal was then signed between the Umayyad Caliphate and the Roman Emperor.

In 717 CE, another Umayyad caliph, Sulayman ibn Abdul Malik, became aware of the political instability in the Roman Empire where three emperors had taken the reins within the span of six years. Sulayman organised a huge army on both land and sea with enormous siege supplies. He appointed his brother, Maslama, as his general. But despite years of preparation and the successful defeat of Byzantine forces across the Middle East, this battle did not favour the Muslims. The dreadful Greek fire, the winter cold and some double-crossing of informants vanquished Muslim chances of capturing Constantinople. Much of the blame for this loss was placed on

Maslama and his war tactics, especially as he'd relied on a Byzantine informant to help him decide the course of the fight. The informant was named Leo who used Maslama to gain personal power in Constantinople rather than aid the Muslim conquest. This defeat was humiliating for the Umayyad Caliphate, and after a short period, a new caliphate, the Abbasid, replaced their rule in 750 CE.

It was during the Abbasid caliphate that the Turkic tribes rose to power. While the caliphate welcomed these Turkic tribes into its cities and army, it didn't realise that one day it would be replaced by the Turks. By the 11th century, much of the Abbasid Caliphate's territory came under the rule of the Seljuk Turks, who came from the many branches of the Oğuz Turks. The Seljuks managed to conquer much of the eastern and central Islamic world, spanning modern Iran, Iraq, northern Syria and its neighbours. It became known as the great Seljuk Sultanate and acquired the title Sultanate of Rum when it acquired the eastern borders of the Byzantine Empire in Asia Minor (then known as Anatolia, now modern Turkey).

The emergence of the Seljuks and their fierce expansion put a dampener on things for the Byzantine Empire. During the Abbasid Caliphate's loss of central power, Byzantium had sought to reclaim its lost territory, but the emergence of the Seljuks meant that the fight against its formidable foe, Islam, continued.

During the 11th century, the Seljuks spotted a weakness in the southern borders of Byzantium in Anatolia. These border towns were not well-defended so the Seljuks pounced and captured many of them. But the Byzantine Emperor, Romanus IV, had had enough of the Seljuk menace and sought to end their incursions. Unbeknown to him, this drive would backfire and initiate the Turkic rise to power in Anatolia.

It began in the Battle of Manzikert (Malazgirt), named after a town in Armenia, north of Lake Van. In 1071 CE, the Seljuk Turks were led into battle by their legendary sultan, Alp Arslan. He had been the first to lead attacks and capture Byzantine towns within the borders of Syria. Emperor Romanus IV had sent peace envoys to broker a treaty, but these emissaries were spies. They gathered information on Arslan's army and fortress and gave the Emperor the confidence to launch his attack.

Alp Arslan's feats were heroic and may have been a great source of inspiration for Mehmed II. Arslan was in the middle of fighting the Shia Fatimid dynasty in Syria when news reached him of Byzantine troops attacking Seljuk towns. (The Shia or Shi'it Ali – the sect of Ali – is a religious group that differs from the mainstream Sunni Islam on ideological and political world view).

Arslan knew how to outsmart his opponents. While Emperor Romanus IV had amassed his troops to end Seljuk rule, it was Arslan who surprised him. The Byzantine army was expecting Arslan to reach Lake Van from the south. However, he surprised them from the north leading his army through a longer, unknown route – crossing Iran and avoiding Byzantine scouts. This surprise attack on 30,000 Byzantine troops had a demoralising effect. Amid the battle, they heard the rumour that their emperor had retreated, leading many Roman soldiers to abandon the battle. Arslan then turned his attention to Manzikert where the rest of Byzantine army and the Emperor were camped. At first, he sent the traditional Islamic offer of peace but the Emperor felt confident that he had the numbers to end the Seljuk menace and rejected it. This did not worry Arslan because he was ready for war. He turned to his second tactic – one that the Turks were famed for: hit and run. Throughout the night and the next day, they pestered the Byzantine army by attacking and retreating as a ploy to separate and isolate the right and centre flanks of the Byzantine army. This strategy helped the Seljuks to encircle and destroy both the right and centre Byzantine flanks. It created a state of chaos among the Byzantine troops and led to an easy capture of Emperor Romanus IV.

The Battle of Manzikert was a humiliating defeat for Romanus IV. But Arslan proved himself a generous victor and signed a peace treaty with the imprisoned Emperor and set him free. The terms of this peace treaty were: 1.5 million gold reparation, an annual tax of

300,000 gold, and four Byzantine cities were to be handed to the Seljuks: Antioch, Edessa, Hierapolis and Manzikert. A dynastic marriage was also signed between the Emperor's daughter and Arslan's son. Emperor Romanus IV then returned to his capital, Constantinople, but within a year he was killed by his own people, making the peace treaty void.

After the Battle of Manzikert, within two decades much of Byzantine's heartland in Anatolia came under Seljuk rule, gaining them the title of the Seljuk of Rum (Roman) and effectively weakening Byzantine military power. The Seljuks rebuilt and restored former Byzantine towns, giving them a distinctive Islamic and Turkic appearance. Byzantine towns that had been tightly enclosed were spread out by the Seljuk, with bazaars, orchards, running water and public fountains. The dominant Islamic features became the mosques (masjids) with medreses (schools), beside which were goldsmiths and bookstores. The mosques also had attached buildings serving as hospitals for mental and physical ailments. In addition, there were several *imaret* or soup kitchens, and lodgings for the poor scattered across the towns.

For another 150 years, the Seljuks grew in power and status but as history often shows, after every rise there is also an eventual fall. By the 13th century, the Seljuks faced the formidable Mongolian hordes. Coming from northern China, the Mongolians had conquered much of the Middle East and besieged and sacked Baghdad in 1258, the capital of the Abbasid Caliphate, causing its downfall. In the plains of Anatolia, the Seljuk Turks fought the Mongolian expansion but were defeated.

The Seljuk rule disintegrated into a dozen Turkic states known as beyliks. From among these beyliks, 'the sons of Osman' or Osmanli, came to replace the Seljuk rule. Osman Gazi (the name Gazi meant 'warrior of Islam') was the son of Ertugrul, a warrior who had led a fierce defence against the Mongols and was rewarded by the Seljuks with some land in northern Anatolia called Söğüt. Ertugrul was not from the Seljuk tribe – he was from the Kayi (also spelt Qayi) Turkic tribe.

The Kayi were more a band of warriors than a traditional tribe. However, like the Seljuks, they were a tribe from the many branches of the Oğuz Turks. During the 12th century, the Kayi had settled in Mahan, the north-eastern frontier of Iran. Their leader was Suleymansah, the father of Ertugrul, who escaped with his band of warriors and three sons as the Mongols invaded the frontiers of Iran. They travelled across Persia, Mesopotamia (modern Iraq) and northern Syria, and when crossing the Euphrates River, Suleymansah drowned. His sons could not then agree on what route to take: two headed to Khurasan, a Mongol territory in modern Iran and Afghanistan, while the third son, Ertugrul, went to Erzerum, north-west of Anatolia. With his band of four hundred followers, he served the Seljuk of Rum against the Byzantine Empire. Upon receiving Söğüt, he became the leader of his tribe at the end of the 13th century. Some coins from the 1270s bear his name but not much more is known about Ertugrul; it was only one hundred years after his death in 1280 that stories emerged about his heroic feats. However, it was his son, Osman Gazi, whose successful defeat of the Byzantine army in 1302 at the Battle of Bapheus, that formed the Osmanli beylik, 'the sons of Osman'. This was later adapted into English as the Ottoman Empire, a derivation of the Arabic name Uthman or Osman, which was referred to in the Islamic world as Caliphate Uthmaniya .

Osman Gazi's rise to power is most popular in legendary tales. Some tales claim that his pursuit of military fame was to win the love of Malkhatun, the daughter of a religious leader, Shaykh Edebali, who approved Osman's betrothal to Malkhatun when he heard Osman's dream. In this legendary dream, Osman had seen a moon rise up from the Shaykh's chest and settle on Osman's chest. Then a tree emerged from Osman's chest, its mighty branches spread across the skies. The roots of this tree gave birth to the four great rivers: the Tigris and Euphrates in Iraq, the Nile in Egypt, and the Danube in

Eastern Europe. The Shaykh considered this dream as a prophecy that Osman and his descendants would be great conquerors and would create a great empire. He saw the moon to be his daughter, Malkhatun, and, pleased with his interpretation, he let her marry Osman.

As the leader of the Kayi tribe, Osman continued in his father Ertugrul's footsteps in pursuing *gazi*: war against the infidels. His first confrontation with the Byzantine Empire took place in 1302 CE at the Battle of Bapheus. The Byzantine emperor, Andronikos II Palaeologus, had sent his army to end Osman's increasing power. However, Osman and his supporters stood their ground and fought to defeat the Byzantine forces. Their resilience, despite their small number facing a mighty empire, turned the tide of victory and gave them the confidence to continue their fight with Byzantium and gain much of its territory.

When Osman died in 1324, his son Orhan succeeded him and continued the fight. Orhan was the first to use the title *sultan*, it was inscribed next to his name in a masjid in Ankara a year after his death. It was also common for the Ottoman leaders to be called *emir* (Arabic for 'commander' or 'prince'). The word sultan in Arabic refers to a 'ruler' but it is originally derived from Aramaic, meaning 'power' and has appeared in several Qur'anic verses often associated with moral authority.

> "Those whom you serve beside Him are merely idle names that you and your fathers have fabricated, without Allah sending down any sanction (sultan) for them. All authority to govern rests only with Allah. He has commanded that you serve none but Him. This is the Right Way of life, though most people are altogether unaware." (Qur'an, Yusuf, 40)

Shortly after his father's death, Orhan captured Prusa, known in Turkish as Bursa, a town in the north-western hills of Anatolia. It was the first Ottoman capital and gave Orhan and his followers a base from which to continue their conquest of the Byzantine territory and the Balkans. In 1329 CE, Orhan laid siege to Nicaea and successfully captured it by 1331 CE. He was able to conquer all of Bithynia, which was on the northwest of Anatolia beside the Sea of Marmara, the Bosphorus and the Black Sea. He also entered central Anatolia, taking power from other beyliks and reached the Dardanelles. In 1333 CE, Ibn Battuta, a Muslim explorer who travelled more than 100,000 km, described Orhan as the *"greatest of Turkoman rulers, the richest in wealth, land and military forces, possessing nearly a hundred fortresses."*

The Byzantine emperor, Cantacuzenus, could only respond by signing a peace treaty with Orhan in 1346 CE and giving him his daughter in marriage. Orhan returned the favour by giving Cantacuzenus military support to fight with Thrace. However, an earthquake in Gallipoli in 1354 left many Byzantine towns abandoned, which Orhan used as an excuse to capture and launch his European campaigns.

Not long after, in 1362, Orhan died and was succeeded by his son Murad I, who continued in his father's gazi footsteps. By 1369, Murad I captured Adrianople, calling it Edrine and using it as his base to launch attacks in the Balkans. During his reign, several European towns and territory came under his control. In 1371, defeating the Serbians in the Battle of Maritza, he entered the Balkans. In 1376, he made Bulgaria an Ottoman vassal. By 1387 he conquered southern Macedonia. The Balkan rulers tried to confront the Ottoman advance by forming a coalition of troops from Serbia, Kosovo and Bosnia. Although Murad I successfully defeated their challenge, he was later assassinated by a soldier. Murad's son, Beyezid I, took over the reins and continued the conquests.

Although Sultan Orhan's descendants managed to encircle the Byzantine Empire, the conquest of its heart, Constantinople, remained out of reach for another 150 years. On four occasions, the Ottomans made serious attacks on Constantinople. These occurred during the reigns of Murad I (1376), Bayezid I (1394–1402), Musa

Çelebi (1411), and Murad II (1422), the father of Mehmed II. These unsuccessful attempts to conquer Constantinople and end the reign of Byzantium may have increased Byzantine morale and confidence. Its impenetrable city walls were its key defence, even though much of its territory was under the rule of the Ottomans.

Mehmed II may have looked up to his great-grandfather, Sultan Bayezid I (r. 1389–1402), and his campaigns on the Byzantine Empire. Bayezid I was the fourth Ottoman sultan. The Turks nicknamed him *Yildirim*, translated as 'Thunderbolt', because his army was swift and constantly on the move between Asia and Europe. He had continued his predecessor's relentless pursuit of conquering Byzantine and European territory. During his reign, Bayezid I conquered most of Serbia, captured the capital of Bulgaria, much of northern Greece, and his Ottoman troops were the first to cross the Danube River to capture Wallachia. His rule covered an area of 670,00 square kilometres.

Although his siege of Constantinople in 1394 was unsuccessful, due to lack of technology as well as dealing with other campaigns, he created a strong Ottoman presence in Europe for his descendants to exploit. Before the siege of Constantinople, he had built the fortress, Guzelcehisar (Beauteous Castle) later called Anadolu Hisari, some 5 km north of Constantinople and aimed to control the Bosphorus.

The European powers called for a crusade in 1396 to end Bayezid's reign. Approximately 100,000 crusaders from Hungary, Wallachia, Germany, Italy, France, Spain, England as well as Genoa, Venice, and the Knights of St. John in Rhodes came to confront the Ottomans. Bayezid was forced to leave the siege of Constantinople and brought his 200,000-strong army to successfully defeat the crusaders in Nicopolis. He gained much praise and acclaim from the Muslim world for this victory and confidently he approached the ceremonial Abbasid Caliph in Cairo to give him the title of 'Sultan of Rum', which the caliph granted. This was also in defiance of Tamerlane who demanded that Bayezid become his subject. Tamerlane was a Mongolian ruler famed for his bloodthirsty conquests across Asia, unlike Bayezid whose conquests established a more enlightened and educated society.

Bayezid's victorious celebration did not last long, as yet again he had to leave the siege of Constantinople to face the encroaching army of Tamerlane. Tamerlane's powerful army besieged Ankara, and after a long battle, he defeated and imprisoned Bayezid. The Ottoman poet Arabshah lyrically lamented Bayezid's tragic death as having *"fallen into the hunter's snare and been confined like a bird in a cage."*

Bayezid's death shattered the Ottoman rule, causing much of its territory to be lost and reclaimed by its rivals, the Christians in Europe and other beyliks in Anatolia. The eight year siege of Constantinople ended and for eleven years, a bloody civil war ensued between Bayezid's four sons. There was no rule of how succession should take place in the Ottoman Empire. It was only left for the strongest son to inherit his father's throne. Eventually, Mehmed II's grandfather, Mehmed I, in 1413, was successful in ending the civil war and reclaimed lost Ottoman territory in Anatolia and the Balkans. Like his predecessors, Mehmed I was unsuccessful in capturing Constantinople. However, he did leave his grandson, Mehmed II, something that would make his army the best. He strengthened the role of the Janissaries, in Turkish pronounced as *yeniçeri*, meaning 'new troops'.

The Janissaries stood out in their white felt caps which originated from the headgear of the Anatolian *gazis*. They were the elite cavalry and infantry soldiers of the Ottoman army. Some claim that Orhan first introduced this force who numbered in the thousands during the rule of Murad I and his son, Bayezid I, who established the *devşirme* (levy of youth) and later Mehmed's grandfather, Mehmed I made the Janissaries the core of the Ottoman army.

Across the Balkan states of Bulgaria, Macedonia, Greece, Serbia, Albania, Bosnia and Herzegovina, official Janissaries travelled to select healthy and intelligent Christian boys between the ages of eight to twenty. It was not a ruthless levy of boys because the sons of widows were not taken, or those who had a single son. Boys who knew Turkish or were street smart orphans were also not taken. Selected boys were brought to Ottoman cities or farms to gain their early education in languages, religion and culture before their military training began. This was a human levy or conscription, known as *devşirme* in Turkish. Although it was not acceptable in Islam to convert by force non-Muslims or to conscript non-Muslims. However, the Ottomans were keen to increase their army size. The training and the career opportunities of a Janissary soon made the Balkan parents eager to have their sons recruited. Some even bribed the officials to accept their sons into the Janissary corps.

While these young boys never lost touch with their families, they, however, adopted Islam as a way of life. They led devout lives both spiritually and physically by keeping hygienic habits and avoiding swearing, quarrelling, gambling, and drinking. It took seven years for these young boys to graduate. These years were spent practising the Islamic values of honesty, loyalty, good manners, and self-control. They also acquired skills in leadership, military, and athletic skills, as well as language, religion, science, and creative arts. The Janissary military training included using bows, slings, crossbows, and javelins. Using these skills, they were an unstoppable force. A sign of their status was to be the best marksman and at the elite level, they were known as head riskers. Later when muskets were introduced, they considered it the weapons of robots and not warriors. A Janissaries' courage was acclaimed and rewarded with pay bonuses and honorary badges known as 'badges of valour' and the shahid's (martyr) family was given financial support.

Upon completion of their training, they were appointed to different posts ranging from page, court official, and eventually some reached the rank of a vezir. Sultan Murad I had decreed sixteen guidelines for the Janissaries to follow; these included: total obedience to the officer; united in their goal; disciplined military conduct; balanced lifestyle and no excesses in luxury or abstinence; observance of religious duties; recruitment of the best soldiers; capital punishment; punishment by own officer; promotion by rank; responsibility over own dependents; no beards for low-ranked soldiers; marriage after retirement; residence in barracks; no other jobs; full-time military service; no alcohol or gambling. It is estimated that during Mehmed II's reign, the Janissaries numbered approximately eight to ten thousand. As an elite fighting force, they were responsible for maintaining order but principally, they lead the decisive events in battle. Their pay was three to five *akçe* (Turkish silver coin) per day and were always well-supplied with uniforms, food, and ammunition. They became very influential and loyal to the sultan, however, they were also known to protest and mutiny. If a kettle was turned upside-down during their mealtime, it was a sign of mutiny.

While many Europeans considered the Janissaries as the most elite branch of the Ottoman army. However, the Ottoman army was organised into several branches with distinct duties and responsibilities. Its most elite branch was the *Kapıkulu* corps, which were the infantry units, while its *sipahi*, cavalry were most effective in winning battles through surrounding and overpowering the enemy. There were also *azap*, the infantry in front of the artillery and in the rear guarding the supplies. The *azaps* were specialised archers who were either conscripts or volunteer infantry. The *akinci*, light cavalry, lured the enemy into an ambush led by the artillery units and Janissaries. These raiders were the Ottoman auxiliary cavalry – a fast-moving and ruthless force feared most by the Europeans. Their aim was to terrorise their enemy by leading raids deep into the enemy lands collecting information, breaking their enemies' communication, and paving the path for the approaching Ottoman army. The *akinci* were famous for controlling the Ottoman boarders, often in mountainous regions, they would engage in guerrilla warfare to destabilise their enemy and curb their resistance.

The Ottoman army was famed for its skilled cavalry, however, there was more to the army than its cavalry's skills and ambushes. It was the strict discipline of the Ottoman army that impressed foreigners and gained them a prestigious mention in history. Their military success was mainly due to their discipline and the order that shaped every aspect of their army through maintaining roads, keeping supplies, and even having support services. The training of the soldiers was strict and disciplined. They trained through games such as throwing javelins from horseback or practising archery. Their diet was basic and being clean was prioritised. This meant that clean and ordered lanterns were found in their camps and no one was to be seen drunk. Their camps were clean and disease free with an unnatural quietness. The Ottomans were also planners and took great strategic care in planning their expeditions. They reviewed the previous battles to learn from their past. Often European literature express much awe of the Ottoman army's discipline, organisation, and effectiveness and consider it as the first professional army. This is well expressed in Bertrandon de la Broquilre, 15th century, description of the Ottoman army camp:

> *"When they are ready and know when the Christians are coming... they leave quickly and in such a manner that a hundred-armed Christians would make more noise leaving their camp than ten thousand Turks. All they do is beat a large drum. Those who are supposed to leave get in front and all the rest fall into line, without breaking up the order... They are diligent and get up early in the morning. They are frugal when on the road and live on only a little food."*

Mehmed II was born into a family of warriors and conquerors. Befittingly, they gave themselves the last name *gazi*, an Arabic word which means 'warrior of the faith'. The title gazi is derived from the word *ghazw*, which referred to the military expeditions led by the Prophet Muhammad and gazi became a title of honour for Muslim warriors. The Ottomans expressed this deep pride in their affiliation with Islam, which inspired Mehmed to defend and establish the Islamic rule across the lands he conquered. Today Mehmed II's sword is on display in the Topkapı Palace Museum, housed in the palace that he built beside the Hagia Sofia after his successful conquest of Constantinople in 1453. What is engraved on his sword illuminates much about his personality and motivation to be a great conqueror. As the seventh sultan of the Ottoman Empire, Mehmed II tried to surpass his ancestors. The text on his sword reads in Arabic calligraphy:

> "In the name of Allah, the most beneficent, the most merciful. Praise be to Allah Almighty who blesseth religious faith with lustrous and lucid verses and sharp and shining swords. Prayers and peace upon our noble Prophet Muhammad and his household who were attributed with the most exquisite lucent words. Bless and strengthen Mehmed II, son of Murad II, the poignant sword that is drawn in the name of jihad, the Sultan of gazis and mujahideen that striveth to glorify the holy men of Allah, may the necks of the enemies of sharia becometh the scabbard of his sword, shed your grace on the ink of his pen.
>
> Son of Osman, son of Orhan, son of Murad, son of Bayezid, son of Mehmed, may Allah cleanse them with the heavenly waters that streameth by the swords of gazis and place them under the shadow of swords in heaven. Amen, O God of the universe."

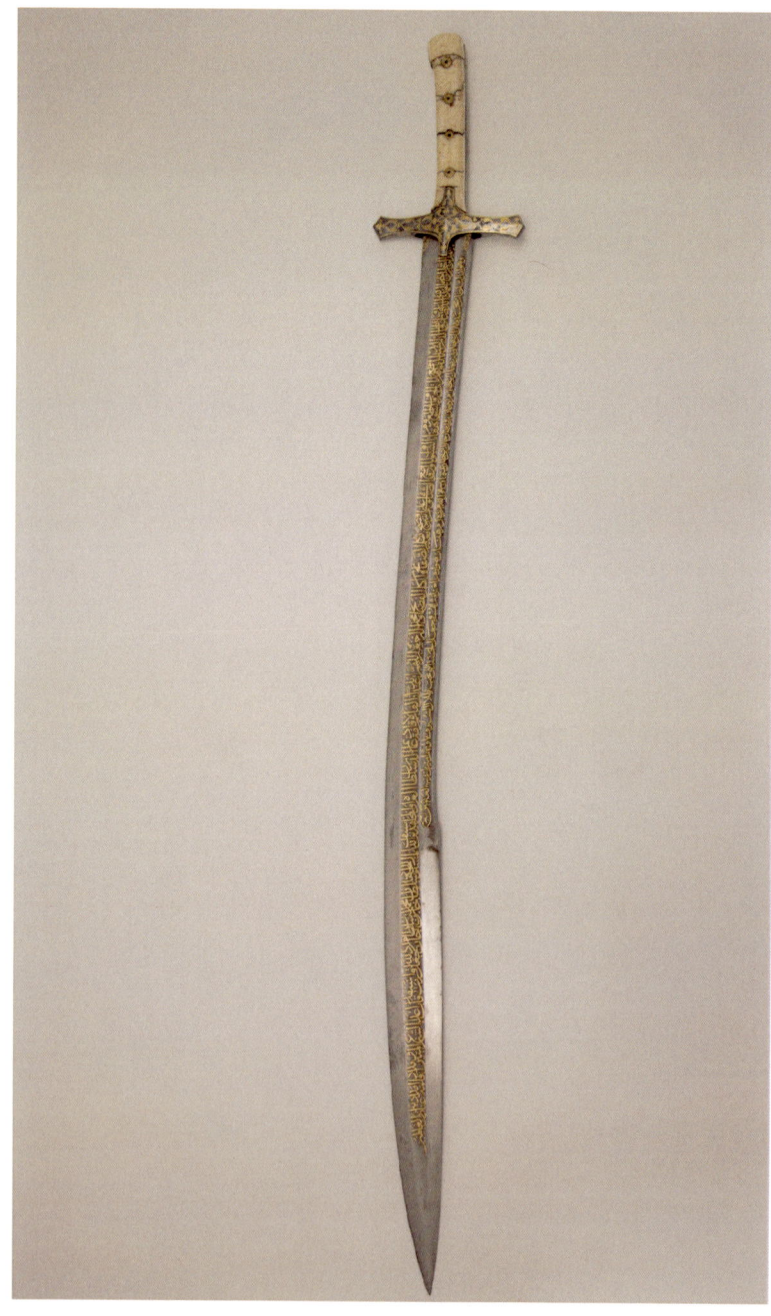

Sultan Mehmed's sword, Topkapı Palace Museum

Chapter 2

MEHMED'S EARLY LIFE

"Your father has sent me to instruct you, but also chastise you, in case you should not obey me." Mullah Gurani

In the quiet of dawn, 30 March 1432, Hatun gave birth to her only child, Mehmed. Oddly enough, it was a year of peace in the Ottoman Empire. Her husband, Sultan Murad II, was spending much of his time in his capital, Edrine, where his son was born. Edrine, originally named Adrianople or Hadrianopolis as it was founded by the Roman emperor, Hadrian, was to the north of Constantinople, close to the borders of Greece and Bulgaria. It became famous for its Ottoman architecture and for ninety years, 1369–1453, it was the Ottoman capital.

There is little known about Mehmed's mother. On two occasions, once on a charitable foundation and on her tomb stone, she was called *Hatun bint Abdullah*, meaning 'distinguished lady, daughter of Abdullah'. But that was not her actual name. Mehmed's mother's name is unknown and there is no record of her lineage or heritage. She was the wife of Sultan Murad II and the mother of his successor. However, that is where our knowledge of her begins and ends. She was known as Hatun, the lady, and her tomb is referred to as *Hatuniya Türbe*.

Hatun lived most of her life in Bursa, the first Ottoman capital, which was famed for its natural beauty. Her life was within the walls of the palace, in the *harem* as it was known. Under Islamic law, women and men were prohibited from intermingling unless they are direct family members such as father, brother, uncle or husband. The aim was to create a pure environment where one was less tempted to see the opposite gender.

Hatun stayed within the walls of the harem and its doors remained closed to outsiders. It was, however, these outsiders who made claims about Hatun's ancestry. Some said that she may have been a European Jew from Italy named Stella, while others have linked her to a Persian princess giving her the name *Huma*, a bird of paradise. The most credible argument remains that bint Abdullah was a common name for former slaves. Her father's name, Abdullah, was commonly used by converts to Islam, which indicate her non-Muslim heritage.

The Harem door at Topkapı Palace, Istanbul

Although her life story may be unrecorded in the archives of history, she will always be known through her son, Sultan Mehmed II, the Conqueror. But how she mothered him, nurtured him, and loved him will never be known. The bond between mother and son, and what role she may have played in the development of his character and personality, will always be subject to speculation.

On the other hand, a wealth of detail is given about Mehmed's father, Sultan Murad II, who ruled the Ottoman Empire for thirty years (1421–44 and 1446–51). Murad II succeeded his father Mehmed I in 1421 at the age of seventeen; however, he was already well-experienced in warfare and the politics of the Ottoman court.

His immediate concern was to deal with the pretenders who tried to topple him from his sultanate. One pretender was the 'false' Mustapha, who claimed to be his uncle, while another claimed to be his brother. Both were supported by the Byzantine emperor, Manual II. This had given Murad II an important reason to lay siege to Constantinople in 1422, which was not successful. For the remainder of his reign, Murad was occupied with extending and securing Ottoman territory, as well as withstanding crusader encroachments.

As the sixth Ottoman sultan, Murad II was most famous for his just leadership. He had spent all his life either defending Ottoman territory or leading wars against its enemies, whether in the west or east. However, he had remained a just and humble ruler, unlike many rulers of the Middle Ages. He ensured the safety and protection of the non-Muslims who lived in Ottoman lands. To live there, they were required to pay an annual tax that guaranteed their protection.

Murad's people enjoyed many privileges throughout his reign. He was very popular and became a father figure to his subjects. His priority was the welfare of his people and he dedicated much of the government's revenue to public buildings and projects. This included building numerous mosques (*camiler*), hospitals, schools (*medreseler*), dining halls for the poor, and roadside inns for travellers known as *kervansaray*.

Murad's army was staunchly loyal to him because he was attuned to their welfare and his policies favoured them. During the siege of the fortress of Kurje in Albania 1450, his adviser had encouraged him to continue with the siege into the winter months. However, Murad famously replied, *"If I attack, many men will be killed. I would not give one of my soldiers for fifty such fortresses."*

Without a doubt, Mehmed II had big shoes to fill. But he didn't need to worry as he was the third in line to the sultanate. Mehmed had two older brothers, who were from different wives of the Sultan.

Islamic law permitted men to have four wives and as many concubines (female slaves captured during war). Ahmed Çelebi was Mehmed's oldest brother; he was born in 1420 to one of Murad's concubines. A child born to a concubine was a legitimate heir according to Islamic law, because the relationship between the concubine and the sultan was like a traditional marriage. Mehmed's second oldest brother, Alaeddin Ali Çelebi, was born in 1425 through his wife, Hadice Hatun. And it was Alaeddin who Murad seemed to admire and favour the most.

Mehmed spend his early childhood in the palace of Edirne, within the *harem* with his mother and wet-nurse, Hundi Hatun. At the age of two, in 1434, he left Edirne and settled in Amasya, where his oldest brother, Ahmed Çelebi, was a governor. It was the norm to appoint the eldest son as the governor, though he was guided by officials who were selected by the sultan. Amasya was situated in the north of Anatolia, close to the Black Sea and was the ideal residence for Murad's heirs. It was a beautiful city surrounded by rugged mountains and adorned by mosques, castles and mountain streams, with lush mulberry gardens. It was most favoured by wealthy Ottomans and its clean, fresh air made it an ideal residence for the princes. In the Turkish language a prince was called *Çelebi*.

It was common for the Ottoman princes to reside and be educated in the interior of Anatolia away from the capital, especially in their early years. Murad relied on this distance to keep his sons safe. Unfortunately, this measure failed for his oldest son. Tragedy struck his family in 1437, when Ahmed Çelebi, at the age of seventeen, died in mysterious circumstances. The details of who was involved or how it happened were never found. At this time Mehmed was only five years old and he had to replace his brother as the governor of Amasya.

It took two years after the tragic death of Ahmed Çelebi for the Ottoman court to hold any festivities. Although somewhat sombre, the year 1439 became a time of festivity and celebration when both Mehmed and his second oldest brother, Alaeddin Ali, were circumcised. Circumcision for males was a religious requirement in Islam, as it follows in the footsteps of Prophet Abraham. During 1439, another celebration took place, which was the marriage of Mehmed's half-sister into a powerful Turkish family. On these occasions, it was customary to hold days of court festivities where scholars, poets and magistrates would give public talks and recitals. However, Sultan Murad had always led a simple reign and tried to keep these occasions less ostentatious.

Once the ceremonies ended, Sultan Murad immediately sent his sons to govern different Ottoman territories. Mehmed was removed from his governorship of Amasya and instead, his brother, Alaeddin, replaced him there. Mehmed was now sent to Manisa, an ancient city that was once occupied by the Persian and Roman Empires; it was situated in western Anatolia, close to the Aegean Sea. Of course, given their young ages, both boys were not alone in their posts, but were supported by a group of Murad's officials.

During Mehmed Çelebi's childhood, Sultan Murad was often preoccupied with protecting Ottoman territory against the crusaders, as well as his eastern enemies. The crusaders were European Christians who waged a holy war against the Muslims from the 11th to 13th centuries, in the hope of capturing Jerusalem, a holy site for Christians, but also for Jews and Muslims. To reach Jerusalem, the crusaders often passed through the plains of Anatolia, pillaging and looting many towns and cities. Murad had numerous spies across the Balkans, Hungary and even Germany, to gather any details of crusader plans to attack. He was also zealous in gaining control of the Balkans as a way to strengthen the Ottoman Empire and disadvantage its key rival, the Hungarians.

When Mehmed was a teenager, he witnessed his father setting off on numerous battles. In 1443, Murad's spies informed him that his brother-in-law, Ibrahim Bey, who was also his staunch eastern enemy, had made an alliance with the Hungarian rulers to end the Ottoman rule. Ibrahim Bey was the ruler of the beylik Karamanid Turkic tribe that reigned over central and eastern Anatolia. His plots did not sit well with Murad. With his new heir, Alaeddin Ali, he gathered a strong force to confront his brother-in-law. Unfortunately for Ibrahim Bey, he could not match Sultan Murad's powerful army. The only means of survival was to surrender and acknowledge Sultan Murad's rule. Some sources claim that Sultan Murad's sister may have convinced her husband, Ibrahim Bey, to surrender.

In this battle, eighteen-year-old Alaeddin Ali Çelebi had stood among the ranks of soldiers like a true warrior and had made his father proud. He had become his father's favourite son. But upon their victorious return, another tragedy befell Murad's household. In mysterious circumstances, Alaeddin and his two infant sons were found dead. They may have been strangled to death. Alaeddin's adviser, Kara Hizir, was accused of their murder, but his motive was never established because he was promptly executed.

Alaeddin's death was a tragedy that Murad never forgot and in his will, he requested that he be buried next to his son and no other family member. His will was written in Arabic on a scroll, which instructed his vezir on how to deal with his burial. It read:

> "When I die, you are to bury my body in Bursa three to four arching (approximately 2 m) from the grave of my son Alaeddin, not far from my mosque. Do not build a sumptuous türbe [tomb] over it, as for great rulers. Lay my corpse directly in the earth. Over me let the rain fall as the grace of God; only build four walls around my grave and set a roof over them, so that the Qur'an readers may sit there. Bury none of my children or relatives beside me..."

Life continued despite this sad event in Mehmed's family. Immediately, Murad called his surviving son, Mehmed, to his palace in Edirne and officially declared him as his sole heir. Mehmed was only eleven years old. He was forced to leave his mother and the picturesque city of Manisa. He had lived in the palace *serai*, which was on mountain slopes, giving him a sweeping vista of the city and its numerous mosques.

At the vulnerable age of eleven, Mehmed faced the serious world of politics. His father's scrutiny was now ever more on him. It seemed that Murad did not approve of Mehmed as he was a rebellious and strong-willed child. None of the tutors that Murad employed could discipline or teach Mehmed. Numerous tutors came and left, unsuccessful in their attempts to guide him.

Murad needed to discipline and educate his surviving heir. He needed Mehmed to be ready for his role as the next sultan. The solution was found in the famed mullah, a religious scholar, by the name of Şerefeddin Ahmad bin Ismail bin Othman, also known as Şerefeddin Mullah Gurani from Kurdistan. Mullah Gurani had written seven books in Arabic on hadith. And was also a scientist who had written about microbes in his book *The Material of Life*, 1456. Upon the insistence of Sultan Murad, he accepted a position in a *medrese* in Bursa, to teach Islamic law, the science of Qur'an and hadith.

Şerefeddin Mullah Gurani's first meeting with Mehmed was memorable but hostile. With the Sultan's approval, he had brought with him a long stick to use as he wished. Holding the stick, the Mullah spoke sternly to Mehmed Çelebi,

> *"Your father has sent me to instruct you, but also chastise you, in case you should not obey me."*

Mehmed, in his youthful insolence, had simply laughed, which did not work in his favour as the Mullah struck him with his stick. The beating may not have inspired Mehmed to be in awe of his teacher, but for the remainder of their relationship, Mehmed held Mullah Gurani in great respect and they developed a father-son relationship. Within a short period of time, Mehmed had learned the Qur'an and hadith and developed a deep appreciation of learning. He had come across the hadith of Prophet Muhammad about the conquest of Constantinople and saw himself as its conqueror. He learned philosophy, Islamic studies, geography, Latin and Greek history and literature. Later, Mehmed was famed for being fluent in several languages, including Turkish, Latin, Arabic, Persian, Greek, and Slavic. Mehmed had several other tutors whom he later appointed during his sultanate as vezirs or high governmental officials, even as heads of *medrese*.

Whilst Mehmed was busy with his studies, his father continued to be occupied with the threat of war from both the west and the east. In 1443, the crusaders tried to reach the Ottoman capital, Edirne. However, the bitter cold, diminishing supplies and the fierce defence of the Ottoman army made the crusaders turn back.

A year later, in 1444, Sultan Murad signed a peace treaty with his foes, the Hungarians and Serbians. It was a ten-year truce signed by the Sultan in Edirne and the Hungarian King Ladislas in Szeged.

The threat of war was a constant presence in the lives of Ottomans. Even though the peace treaty was signed with the Hungarian, the people of Edirne strengthened their fortifications and some wealthy merchants left for Bursa. When their western borders became peaceful, their eastern neighbours tried to challenge the Ottoman rule. The Karamanid ruler, Ibrahim Bey, tried to revolt yet again. Murad immediately gathered his forces to confront his brother-in-law. He left Mehmed as his deputy in Edirne but it didn't take long for Ibrahim Bey to surrender.

Meanwhile, Mehmed, merely twelve years old, faced his own challenges in Edirne. While the vezir never left his side, Mehmed had to deal with a troublesome commotion caused by a heretic from Persia who was accused of propagating unorthodox beliefs. Some claim that Mehmed may have given this man sanctuary but the populace of Edirne were up in arms demanding his execution, which they managed to achieve. It was ever more obvious to young Mehmed of the challenges of pleasing the population.

After dealing with Ibrahim Bey, Murad turned back to Edirne but on his way, he stopped at Bursa to visit his son, Alaeddin's grave. And upon returning to his court, he made a surprising announcement to his vezirs. He was stepping down from his sultanate and giving the reins to his son, Mehmed. Whether it was due to Alaeddin's death or his own austere lifestyle, Murad never gave a reason for his abdication. And his grand vezirs could not persuade him to reconsider his decision. His declaration was clear:

> *"I have given my all – my crown, my throne to my son, whom you should recognise as Sultan."*

Chapter 3

A YOUNG SULTAN

"(Mehmed) forged his bold plans ... with youthful impetuosity and daring, a sharp and penetrating judgement uncommon for his age ... he was far superior ... in military talent and political insight and skill." Franz Babinger

By early December 1444, Mehmed Çelebi was announced as the new sultan; he was only twelve-and-a-half years old. However, Murad was not so indifferent to the future of the Ottoman empire. He had left his trusted advisers, Halil Pasha, the grand vezir, and Mullah Husrev, the army judge, to support and guide his son. Murad then turned to a peaceful life of retirement in the city of Manisa where his son had been the governor.

A twelve-year-old sultan undoubtably caused the grand vezir, Çandarlı Halil Pasha, much grievance. He believed that the Ottoman enemies would take advantage of this inexperienced boy. And his fear proved true as King Ladislas of Hungary, not even a year into the peace treaty that had been signed in Szeged 1444, disregarded his promise. Instead, he gathered his army together with other nobles such as John Hunyadi and the Roman Cardinal Cesarini, and marched towards Edirne.

News of this crusade reached Mehmed, prompting the vezirs to send a letter to his father, Murad, who quickly mobilised his troops and headed towards Edirne. By the time he reached the Bosphorus, he had gathered some 80,000 soldiers, four times outnumbering the Christian soldiers. In the dead of the night, his troops crossed the Bosphorus from Anadolu Hisarı, also called *Akce Hisar*, or *Guzel*, the White or Beautiful Castle. This fort had been built by Mehmed's great-grandfather, Bayezid I in 1395. Murad realised that his soldiers needed help to cross the strait and he promised the locals a gold coin for anyone who helped a soldier pass through this strait. The local Christians and even the Genoese and Venetian sea captains took advantage of this golden opportunity to enrich their pockets. A few kilometres south of the strait, the Byzantine emperor silently saw this spectacle and did not antagonise his Ottoman foes by mobilising his army against them. The Byzantine Empire's basic survival was at stake because much of its territory was either encircled or captured by the Ottomans.

Once in Edirne, Murad headed north with his troops towards Varna, a city in Bulgaria. Varna was nicknamed 'the Pearl of the Black Sea' or the 'Sea Capital of Bulgaria' because of its prime location for trade and its links to Europe. Murad left Mehmed behind with the grand vezir, Halil Pasha, to watch the capital as he was too young to participate in this battle.

On 10 November 1444, Murad's army reached the crusader camp on the Black Sea close to Varna. Silence greeted both camps as the armies stood facing each other across an open field for three hours. The battle did not begin well for the Christian camp as their site was less advantageous. There were no fleets by the Black Sea to aid them and their only escape was through treacherous terrain. Added to their misfortunes was a violent storm that had battered their camp.

Murad ordered a full attack that was successful in weakening the right wing of the crusaders, but the crusaders managed to counter-attack and weaken both wings of the Muslim forces. However, the

Janissaries stood firm and fierce in their resistance. The crusaders' chances of winning further diminished when the old rivalry between their leaders reared its ugly head. The Hungarian King tried to prove himself and led an attack against Murad's infantry. It created a desperate situation on both sides, but the Janissaries managed to withstand the assault and instead killed King Ladislas, who had fallen from his horse. He had his head severed and displayed. Panic ensued among the crusaders causing many troops to escape the battle ending the crusade in disarray. The Ottoman troops joked that the crusaders fled 'like sheep fleeing a wolf'.

The Battle of Varna in 1444 was a serious defeat for the crusaders and made them lose hope of vanquishing the Ottomans and diminishing their threat to Europe. Murad sent triumphant letters to the Muslim world announcing this decisive victory. The Christians also saw their defeat as sacrilegious as the Hungarian king had broken his truce with Murad; he had sworn on the Bible in Szeged. Meanwhile, the Byzantine Emperor, John VIII, tried to appease the Ottomans and immediately sent Murad gifts.

Murad returned victorious but this did not persuade him to take back the leadership from his son; he continued his retirement in Manisa. Although Mehmed signed a peace treaty with Venice, which revived the 1430 treaty conditions that Murad had agreed on, Mehmed did nothing else momentous during his young sultanate; perhaps his vezirs held the reins tight.

It never sat well with Halil Pasha that a twelve-year-old was a sultan and he persisted in finding a way to persuade Murad to return. He took grievances when the Janissaries demanded a pay rise and mutinied when their demands were not met. They allegedly set ablaze several places in the capital, which had reached the bazaar where several merchants had lost their lives. Mehmed put the uprising to rest by promising the Janissaries a pay increase, which was something that Halil Pasha opposed. Rumours spread that Halil Pasha had encouraged the uprising due to his dislike of Mehmed's close adviser, the eunuch, Sihabeddin Pasha, who was non-Turkish.

There was a rivalry and animosity between the old Turks and the Christian converts to Islam. The Ottoman court was famed for being a meritocracy, but some Turks hated the high ranks that were given to the new Muslims, despite their skill and contribution.

On May 1446, the grand vezir's persistence won, and Halil Pasha managed to convince Mehmed to urgently ask his father to return to Edirne and reclaim his capital. What may have been the last straw was Mehmed's desire to launch an attack on Constantinople, which Halil Pasha was not in favour of.

When Murad returned to his throne, he was met enthusiastically by both his people and officials, especially by the Janissaries. His son was nowhere to be seen because Halil Pasha had sent him on a hunting expedition. His father's return to power meant that Mehmed Çelebi withdrew from Edirne and took residence in the palace in Manisa with some of his close companions.

Once in power, Murad recognised the treaty that was drawn by his son with the Venetians. This ensured that the western Ottoman territories did not face any immediate attacks. In addition, his Serbian father-in-law, George Brankovic, maintained peaceful relations. Friendly relations also continued with the Byzantine Emperor, John VIII. And Hungary posed no threat.

Murad then turned his attention to counter-attacking Greece and Albania; both had taken some Ottoman territory during his absence. His plan was also to quash any Byzantine attempts to extend its power north of the Greek isthmus (peninsula).

As always, Murad led a large army with numerous caravans and camels. The Greek cities knew that all their resistance could not match Murad's cannons and mines which toppled one Greek town after another. The ancient city of Corinth fell to the Turks, as well as Sikion and Aiyion, leaving the isthmus without any protection. Approximately 60,000 Greeks were now under Ottoman rule and an enormous amount of valuable goods were seized. When Murad's army reached north of the isthmus, where the city of Thebes lay, the immediate response of Thebes' ruler was to pay tribute tax and accept Ottoman rule without any resistance. By 1446, the Greeks could no longer organise an army to challenge the Ottoman rule.

This stunning victory in Greece was not witnessed by Mehmed Çelebi who had remained in Manisa and not taken any part in the battles. The quiet pace of life in Manisa, however, did not match his own. Mehmed had been busy supporting Turkish pirates in the Aegean Sea who were wreaking havoc across the Aegean islands. And indirectly, he was waging a war against the Greeks. Mehmed was only sixteen and had not seen the need to consult his father on this quest. He had taken the initiative himself and given these pirates the go ahead to raid and cause chaos that would benefit the Ottomans.

By 1448, Mehmed's life was becoming more interesting. At the age of sixteen, his first son was born through his concubine, Gülbahar. He named him Bayezid. Legend links his concubine, Gülbahar bint Abdullah, to French royalty, but she may have been a Christian slave from Albania. She bore his son in an old Byzantine castle called Thracian Dimotika; it was not only used as a residence for the sultan's family, but it was also an Ottoman treasury. But Mehmed could not remain with his young family for long. Sultan Murad had ordered him to join him in Edirne, to prepare for the Albanian campaign, and bring copper, tin and cannon igniters with him.

The crusade leader, John Hunyadi, had not forgotten the humiliation of the Battle of Varna and so he gathered troops to face the Ottomans yet again and end their threat. Once Murad was aware of the Hungarian advance, he quickly mobilised his troops and immediately set off to Bulgaria to prevent them from crossing the mountains. Turkish sources report approximately 50,000 to 60,000 soldiers while Christian sources exaggerate this number to 150,000. Upon the plains of Kosovo, both sides met.

The campaign against the Hungarians was Mehmed Çelebi's first battle. His father stood with his Janissaries watching Mehmed on the battlefield alongside the Anatolian troops on the right. His Rumelian troops (the Ottoman soldiers from Europe) attacked from the left and the auxiliary soldiers, known as *azaps*, guarded the front lines. The Hungarians organised their troops into thirty-eight lines to compensate for their lack of numbers. The Ottomans attacked the Hungarian forces from the rear and their larger force gave them a decisive victory causing John Hunyadi to hastly retreat. The loss in both Varna and Kosovo damaged Hunyadi's reputation and made him lose favour with the Pope.

Mehmed returned to Edirne without any battle scars but with the taste of victory. On his return, his father decided to arrange his son's marriage into a wealthy Turkoman family. Mehmed was now seventeen, and it was tradition to marry at this age. The Sultan sought one of the hands of Süleyman Bey's beautiful daughters. Süleyman Bey ruled the interior of Asia Minor with his large and loyal army, he was part of the Karamanid Turkoman tribe. His great wealth had grown through trading horses as he was an excellent horseman. Like Murad's own marriages, these unions were really for the sake of strengthening the Ottoman Empire and removing its political rivals.

Mehmed's chosen bride was brought to Edirne with great pomp and ceremony. One of the vezirs' wives had visited Süleyman Bey's harem and selected Sitt Hatun, his most beautiful daughter. Upon her father's acceptance of the proposal, the vezir's wife kissed her eyes and gifted her with jewels. Her cortège travelled through the mountains of Anatolia. A procession nobles and scholars lined the streets of Bursa welcoming her into the Ottoman family.

The wedding day was no less grand. It was celebrated for three months with traditional festivals that included poetry recitals and competitions. Once the celebrations ended, Mehmed took his bride with him to Manisa. It is unknown whether Mehmed had any love for his arranged bride, but for the remainder of their lives they lived in different cities. In April 1467, she died without bearing any of his children.

A year after having his first child and getting married, Mehmed faced the loss of his mother, who died in 1449. She was buried in

Bursa, in the Hatuniye Türbe, 90 m away from her husband's grave and just two years before his death. It is interesting that her tombstone was commissioned by Mehmed rather than her husband. The Arabic inscription describes her as a *'queen among women'*, which gives us some insight into the honour that Mehmed bestowed upon his mother. His tone also gives the impression that he is already a sultan. Murad did not publicly react to this, but he may have secretly enjoyed witnessing his son's ambition. Her tomb inscription reads in Arabic:

> *"Praise be to God! This illustrious tomb was erected in the days of our lord, the mighty sultan, the exalted Hakan, the sultan and sultan's son, Murad, son of Mehmed, son of Bayezid Khan – the noble lord, the sultan Mehmed-Sultan – may God fasten the strap of his authority to the pegs of eternity and reinforce the supports of his power until the predestined day! – for his deceased mother, queen among women – May the earth of her grave be fragrant! The completion fell in the month of Rejeb, the unique, in the year 853 (mid-September 1449)."*

The year 1449 was quieter for Murad. He spent much of his time on an island called Tunca, close to Edirne, keeping only company with scholars. However, it was a different story for Mehmed as he was becoming a force to be reckoned with. From Manisa, he sent out his pirates to raid Venetians in the Aegean Sea coast. The Venetian senate expressed much rage and frustration over these raids. They bewailed that "for three years without any interruption" the Turkoman pirates attacked the island under the direct orders of the Sultan's son. Mehmed Çelebi was acting as if Manisa was his seat of government and he could rule the land and sea independently of his father. He went a step further in his bid to prove he would be the next sultan. He ordered coins minted with his emblem. The emblem was a monster, like a legendary basilisk, coiled menacingly as a snake, or a royal dragon that could kill its victims with a mere glance.

Murad did not react publicly to his son's ambitious zeal. In fact, relations were slowly changing between father and son. A bond was growing between them, perhaps it had something to do with the the fact that they were spending more time together, and that Mehmed was now older and was becoming a man. It was during 1450, that Mehmed had his second son, Mustafa Çelebi. Nothing is known about his mother, but she wasn't Sitt Hatun. It must have been either Gülbahar or his other wife, Gülsah Hatun.

During the same year, Murad was not having much success in his Albanian campaign, so he decided to mobilise his army with Mehmed and lead his soldiers personally. A five-month siege produced no positive results; even 180 kg stone balls hurled at the Krujë fortress could not defeat the Albanians. Bribery and all negotiations to bring about their surrender failed. Finally, Murad decided to withdraw his troops as the ghastly winter had approached. The reaction from the Europeans was joyous celebrations especially as they found a hero who had stood up to the Ottoman advance. His name was Skanderbeg, the defender of Albania, and he now replaced John Hunyadi. For the next decade and a half, Skanderberg remained a staunch Ottoman rival.

Murad returned from Albania to the peaceful solitude of the Tunca island where he began to build his palace. But within a month, he died unexpectedly on February 3, 1451 (855 Islamic New Year). He was only forty-seven years old. Doukas, a Byzantine historian of the 15th century, wrote an admirable eulogy about him:

"Murad kept his given word and not only to those of his own people and faith, for he never violated the treaties he had concluded with the Christians; when the Christians transgressed against the treaties and broke their given word, this did not escape the eye of God, which sees the truth. His just punishment befell them. But His wrath was not long-lived, for the barbarian did not follow up his victories. He did not desire the total destruction of any people. And when the defeated sent envoys to sue for peace, he gave them a friendly reception,

granted their plea, laid down the sword, and went the ways of peace. For this reason also the Father of Peace granted him to die in peace and not by the violence of the sword."

Mehmed learned about his father's death whilst he was in Manisa. A messenger secretly brought the letter from Halil Pasha, because it was feared that a potential attack could prevent Mehmed's accession. It was common for a transition to power to entail some sort of conflict as rivals would take the opportunity to pounce and declare themselves as ruler. For thirteen days Murad's death was kept secret. Stealthily Mehmed mounted his Arabian stallion and commenced his journey to Edirne, exhorting his close companions, *"those who love me follow me"*.

Once in Edirne, Mehmed's presence was kept a secret for a further three days. Then he made a grand entrance into the capital escorted by his close advisers. The people lined the streets, joined by officials, vezirs, the nobility, scholars and now his soldiers, they all welcomed him as the new ruler. His new aides came to kiss his hand and salute his sultanate. Whilst all his advisers were standing around, some vezirs remained at a distance and he called to them. *"Why do my vezirs stand aloof?"* And then he turned to his closest adviser, Sihabeddin Pasha and said, *"Call them, and tell Halil Pasha to take his accustomed place. But as for Ishak, let him as governor of Anatolia accompany my father's corpse to Bursa."*

It had been Halil Pasha who not long go removed Mehmed from his post. And their animosity would eventually take a deadly course. However, Mehmed showed astute leadership and kept Halil Pasha close, reinstating him as the grand vezir. He was only nineteen years old, but he was well aware that he needed to keep the vezirs within his close circle, enabling him to stamp his authority within the Ottoman court and across the Empire.

Mehmed's immediate concern were his foreign enemies. He initiated several peace treaties with Christian leaders to secure Ottoman borders. One of Mehmed's missions was to secure a peace treaty with

Serbia. He relied on his stepmother, Mara, the daughter of the Serbian ruler, to easily achieve this objective. After the death of Murad, he let his stepmother return to Serbia. Once there, the Byzantine Emperor's brother proposed marriage to her, but she refused because she remained a loyal supporter of Mehmed and even spied for him.

Mehmed then tried to keep the rest of the European powers quiet. He made a three-year truce with John Hunyadi, the Hungarian ruler. The Western leaders did not think much of Mehmed; his youth and inexperience did not worry them. Mehmed's eagerness to seek treaties increased their confidence. At the same time, Mehmed need not have worried because of the deep animosity that existed between the Catholic and Orthodox church. This made it highly unlikely that any new crusade would be launched against the Ottoman Empire. Byzantium especially did not want the Catholic church in any way near Constantinople. The Catholic crusader attack and brutal occupation of Constantinople during 1204 to 1261 was never far from their memory. Although some European leaders did make a call for a crusade, it was more of an attempt to rule Constantinople than defeat the Ottomans.

Meanwhile, the Byzantine Emperor, Constantine XI, tried to continue peaceful relations with the Ottomans. He hastily sent his ambassadors to congratulate Mehmed. Mehmed's response was to accept their offers of peace and promise their safety and protection. He also went a step further by promising to send an annual allowance to Prince Orhan, who lived in exile in Constantinople and was his second cousin.

Once Mehmed was satisfied that the Western countries posed little threat to the Ottoman Empire. He had to deal with Ibrahim Bey, the long-time nemesis of the Ottomans, who saw this change of leadership as an opportunity to launch an attack against the Empire. Ibrahim Bey found three young men who claimed that their Ottoman ancestry giving them the right to rule. They gathered a large army and attacked and occupied Ottoman fortresses in Asia Minor.

Sultan Mehmed

Mehmed ordered his vezir, Ishak Pasha, to put an immediate end to this rebellion.

But he also took matters into his own hands by gathering his soldiers and setting out to personally confront Ibrahim Bey. After visiting his father's grave to pay his respects, he turned his army to face his enemy, the Karaman. Mehmed's army met little resistance in recapturing the Ottoman fortresses. Easily defeated, Ibrahim Bey escaped to the Anatolian heartland and sent letters of reconciliation and surrender. Mehmed accepted his pleas and made sure that the Ottoman territories remained under his sultanate.

Defeating Ibrahim Bey had been easy and Mehmed returned victorious in his very first campaign as a sultan. However, it did not take long for new tensions to challenge his leadership. His Janissaries in Bursa demanded increased wages. Mehmed had no choice but to accept their demands. However, he turned his frustrations on the general (*agha*) of the Janissaries and removed him immediately for not maintaining order. He also punished several captains for not disciplining their troops. He decided then that the only way he could stop any future mutiny was if he reordered the numbers of the Janissaries, which would keep them under tighter control.

By now, Mehmed was displaying natural leadership. After returning from the Karaman expedition, he received a letter from the Byzantine Emperor, Constantine XI, demanding that Prince Orhan's allowance be doubled. Prince Orhan was in exile in Constantinople and claimed that his Ottoman lineage entitled him to the sultanate. In this letter, the Byzantine Emperor threatened that if these demands were not met, then the Byzantine Empire would make sure that Orhan would be the next Ottoman sultan. Before Mehmed could reply to their demands, Halil Pasha surprised him with a now famous speech:

> *"You stupid Greeks, I have known your cunning ways for long enough. The late sultan [Murad] was a lenient and conscientious friend to you. The present sultan Mehmed is not of the same mind. If*

Constantinople eludes his bold and impetuous grip, it will only be because God continues to overlook your devious and wicked schemes.

You are fools to think that you can frighten us with your fantasies when the ink on our recent treaty of peace is barely dry. We are not children without strength or sense. If you think that you can start something, do so. If you want to proclaim Orhan as sultan in Thrace, go ahead. If you want to bring the Hungarians across the Danube, let them come. If you want to recover places that you lost long since, try it. But know this: you will make no headway in any of these things. All that you will do is lose what little you have."

Mehmed's reaction was more polite and reserved. He calmly gave them a friendly assurance that once in Edirne he would reply to the Emperor. But on his way there, Mehmed's path was unexpectedly blocked by Christian ships. They had blocked the Gelibolu strait, which prevented Mehmed's soldiers from crossing. He and his army were forced to take a longer passage and cross the Bosphorus through the Anadolu Hisarı. Keeping his anger to himself, he began to plan his own fortress, which became known as the throat cutter or Rumeli Hisarı, directly opposite his great-grandfather's.

Once reaching Edirne in 1451, Mehmed showed how serious he could get. He immediately confiscated all the allowance money for Prince Orhan and ordered that the Ottoman cities with Greek populations be expelled and sent to Byzantium. The tension between the two empires became palpable but Mehmed showed an uncanny calmness as he quietly took residence in his father's palace on Tunca island. The modern historian, Babinger, gives a vivid description of Mehmed inside this castle:

"In the throne room Mehmed received foreign emissaries; in the palace of Cihan-numa he took council with his advisers and associated with scholars, poets, and theologians. It was there that he forged his bold plans which always disclosed, side by side with youthful

Sultan Mehmed

impetuosity and daring, a sharp and penetrating judgement uncommon for his age and which soon made it clear that he was far superior to most of his predecessors and contemporaries in military talent and political insight and skill. It was here no doubt that shortly after his accession he surrounded himself with a number of Occidentals (westerners), especially Italians. His favourite topic of conversation was the heroes of antiquity whom he had decided to emulate, but he also liked to question his guests about conditions in the Christian world."

Chapter 4

THE CONQUEST OF CONSTANTINOPLE

"Verily you shall conquer Constantinople. What a wonderful leader will her leader be, and what a wonderful army will that army be!" Prophet Muhammad

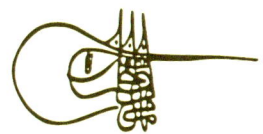

For centuries Constantinople eluded the Muslim conquerors. The Muslims besieged the city on seven different occasions. As the defeats mounted, the allure of this city became legendary. Several of the Prophet Muhammad's hadith had encouraged the conquest of this Roman capital, Byzantium. The Prophet had promised forgiveness for the first army that attacked this city, and he had prophesied that a great leader and a great army would eventually conquer it.

Mehmed became a sultan after his ancestors had already ruled for 150 years and had gained much territory and prestige across the plateaus of Anatolia. They had captured many Byzantine cities and had successfully encircled Constantinople; slowly draining and choking its power, its conquest, however, evaded them. There was tension, rivalry and mistrust between the Ottomans and Byzantines often surfacing when the superficial peace didn't suit their plans. The Byzantine emperor's allegiance to Prince Orhan as the new heir, rather than Mehmed II, hardened Mehmed's resolve to end Byzantine's rule and conquer Constantinople. Their demand of doubling Orhan's allowance was simply a declaration of war that Mehmed clearly welcomed.

Mehmed's war preparation became legendary. It was unlike any other previous campaigns to breach the city's impressive walls. As the winter of 1451 approached, he ordered his men to gather a thousand masons and a thousand limestone workmen. His first plan was to build a fort within four months.

News of his plan reached Constantinople, creating panic among its populace who saw it as a sign of their end, foreshadowing judgement day. The Byzantine Emperor immediately sent representatives to remind Mehmed that his great-grandfather had asked the Byzantine emperor for permission before building the Anadolu fortress, just "like a son requests his father". But Mehmed ignored their pleas. He told them that he was merely controlling his dominions in both Asia and Europe and didn't want to be surprised by his enemies. Mehmed was 19 years old and he didn't shy away from destroying the remnants of the Roman Empire. He confidently told them:

> "I have no intention to do you any injustice, O Romans, ... but only to protect my possessions while doing no injury to you. It is, however, just and right for each of us to guard and make sure of his own... But, as you see, I rule over both Asia and Europe, and in each of these I have many opponents and enemies. I am obliged to be present everywhere and to be equal to the needs of both continents if I do not wish to be taken by surprise... the Italian triremes gave us many great difficulties in the days of my father when we wished to cross against the Hungarians who were attacking us - they prevented us from crossing. We must therefore stop this threat ... So you must not interfere too much. If you enjoy peace, and if you have no intention on your part of preventing us from having this crossing-place, I on my part will neither break my pledges nor desire to do so, provided you will stay in

your own place and not meddle at all in our affairs nor wish to be too prying."

Rumeli Hisari, built in 1452

In March 1452, Mehmed left Edirne to build his fort, Rumeli Hisarı. He brought with him six galleys, eighteen galleons and sixteen supply ships. After studying the land and measuring the strait he chose a legendary site. It was said that this was where Darius, the Persian King, had built his bridge to reach Europe and defeat the ancient Greeks. The fort faced the strait of the Bosphorus that was a kilometre wide with swift currents and was some five kilometres north of Constantinople. Mehmed engineered the plans of his fortress, using stakes he showed his men where to build its towers, bastions, and gates. His fort would house 4000 soldiers and would block the supply ships from reaching Constantinople.

Mehmed ordered his officials to join some 5000 men and begin this remarkable construction. Materials were gathered from across Anatolia: lime, ovens, beams, and stone; some materials were even taken from abandoned churches and ancient temples. He ordered four towers to be built by each vezir, and Mehmed personally helped build the walls connecting the towers. The fort was positioned atop a steep hill, shaped like a triangle, the highest tower reaching 60 meters above the sea with a pointed lead roof. The walls were several meters thick, reaching highest of 15 meters. These walls were modern fortification that could withstand gunpowder warfare. The Byzantines tried to halt its progress by picking fights with the workmen or even imprisoning any Turks found near the walls of Constantinople. When all threats failed, the Emperor decided to appease Mehmed by sending him and his men gifts and food.

A tower built by Mehmed's vezir

A bird's eye view of the fortress shows the shape of the Prophet Muhammad's name in Arabic. On August 31, 1452, the magnificent fort was complete and contained an array of arsenal from javelins, spears, bows, helmets, to shields, crossbows, and cannons. Mehmed appointed Firuz Bey as its commander. His orders were to stop all ships crossing the Bosphorus to pay a toll. If the ships refused, they were to be sunk by the huge brass cannons that were placed on the shore. These cannons could fire 300 kg stone missiles.

The builders and the Greeks called Rumeli Hisarı frightening nicknames: *Bogaz Kesey*, 'cutter of the strait' or *Laimokopia*, 'throat cutter'. Today, cannon balls that weigh 200 kg are still found on the shores of Rumeli Hisarı. At the end of 1452, three Venetian ships refused to pay the toll and lower their sails. Two of these ships managed to escape the wrath of this new cannon, but the third ship sank; all its sailors and its captain were imprisoned and brutally executed.

View of the Bosphorus from Rumeli Hisarı.

Mehmed's war with Byzantine had begun. He left Rumali Hisarı well supplied and on his way to Edrine, he inspected some troops that were positioned along the walls of Constantinople. For three days, he walked along the trenches and gathered the information he needed to accomplish the conquest.

Rumeli Hisarı and its powerful cannon created a state of panic in Byzantium and the rest of Christendom, particularly in Venice and Genoa. It was obvious to all that this was a direct declaration of war. This intense panic was most felt in Constantinople; all grain from the countryside was confiscated and all the surrounding villagers sought refuge within the city walls.

A tower built by Mehmed's vezir

15th century cannon beside the wall of Rumeli Hisarı

Access to Constantinople was becoming more desperate as it depended on European powers for supplies, especially for troops. The Byzantine Emperor could no longer depend on his allies for help. His promises of abundant gold and silver could not persuade them to send reinforcements. The only conditional support was through the Pope's proposal for the union of the Orthodox and Catholic Church. There was a bitter political and theological history between the two which had resulted in the great schism of 1054 and it was unlikely that the two churches would unite. The Orthodox priests and monks found the union abhorrent and preferred Ottoman rule rather than that of the Catholic Church.

Prior to laying siege to Constantinople, Mehmed had made sure that his western enemies and any threat they posed would be controlled during the siege. The only power who posed any possible threat was Hungary. Immediately after his ascension in 1451, Mehmed had sent a friendly message to the Hungarian ruler to establish a truce for three years. In 1452, he went a step further: to distract his enemies from the siege, he spread the rumour that he was pursuing an attack on Hungary. The Christian courts became apprehensive. Mehmed sent his spies to see what their plans were and whether any expeditions were heading his way. He then gained comfort from the news that the Christians were too busy with their internal squabbles to have the foresight to gather their armies against him. Nevertheless, the construction of Rumeli Hisarı ensured that no attack could be brought through the Black Sea.

Unbeknown to Mehmed, secret talks were taking place between Emperor Constantine XI and John Hunyadi. They discussed what support Hungary would offer if Constantinople was attacked. However, their negotiations failed because Hungary demanded to position its troops in two Byzantine locations and insisted on sovereignty over them. The Byzantine Emperor refused the Hungarian demands, but by 1453, the situation was desperate and the Byzantine Emperor was forced to accept Hungarian demands. By that time, however, it was too late as the territories that the Hungarians wanted had already been taken by Mehmed's conquering forces.

At the same time, John Hunyadi was no longer regent of Hungary and he sent an envoy to inform Mehmed that he was not bound by the treaty because the three-year truce had been declared null and void. But Mehmed remained silent and did not immediately respond because the conquest of Constantinople would make everything else much easier.

Meanwhile, once the Bosphorus strait was under his control, Mehmed ordered his general, Turahan Bey and his sons to attack and besiege Emperor Constantine's brother in the Peloponnese. His aim was to make Emperor Constantine XI lose all hope of support. Mehmed's plan was not only successful, leading to several Greek towns being captured, but it also prevented any Greek troops from reaching Constantinople.

Sultan Mehmed knew that the Rumeli Hisarı was not enough to threaten and defeat the Byzantine Empire. He believed that the winning weapon would be the strongest cannon. He had heard about the famous cannon engineer, Urban, who came from Transylvania and had been seeking employment by the Byzantines. However, the Byzantine Emperor could not meet his high wages and Urban had left Constantinople. Mehmed's officials found Urban and offered him double the wages and showered him with gifts on the condition that he design a cannon that could shatter the walls of Constantinople. Urban did not hesitate and agreed to the Mehmed's wishes, but he expressed his doubts about the projectile range of the cannons. Mehmed was not deterred by Urban's concerns. He promptly ordered Urban to start and the problem with the trajectory would be dealt with later. Urban successfully constructed this monster, which could hurl 450 kg projectiles.

This mighty cannon was placed before the *Cihan-numa* palace in Edirne to give its people a sense of security and ease the panic that wartime had created. When this mighty cannon was fired for the first time, its ear-shattering explosion could be heard across Edirne. Its projectile landed more than a kilometre away, creating a 2 m deep hole.

Sultan Mehmed

Dardanelles Gun, 15th century bronze muzzle-loading cannon used in the siege of Constantinople, 1453. Today on display at Fort Nelson, United Kingdom

The Dardanelles Gun, 1453, on display at Fort Nelson, United Kingdom

Mehmed then called a war council and gave an encouraging speech to his nobles, governors, and army generals, majors, and captains to end the Roman Empire:

> "My friends and men of my empire! You all know very well that our forefathers secured this kingdom...(a) proof of their courage in danger... firmness of purpose... and hope to secure complete power over Asia and Europe... they made themselves masters of this region... nothing was any obstacle to them... From that time to the present, (this) city has unceasingly and constantly plotted against us, and our own people against each other, created disorders, and disturbed and injured our realm... plots against our power, should we hesitate and do nothing?"
>
> "Let us not then delay any longer, but let us attack the City swiftly with all our powers and with this conviction: that we shall either capture it with one blow or shall never withdraw from it, even if we must die, until we become masters of it.
>
> "And I myself will first of all be with you and gladly share your travails, and will direct everything in the best way. I will reward the brave with appropriate gifts, each after his worth and valour, according as each is conspicuous in danger or distinguished for some special exploits."

Mehmed reminded his men of his great-grandfather, Bayizad's siege, which was only held back by the crusades and Tamerlane's attack. While his own father, Murad II had the city within his hand but was discouraged by his advisers to withdraw. Now, he stressed was the ideal time for Constantinople's conquest because it had lost much of its glory, emptied of its people, and cut off by the sea. His zealous speech received a rousing agreement and enthusiasm.

It took two months, from February to March 1453, to transport the heavy Ottoman weaponry from Edirne to Constantinople. Usually, it would take troops a mere two days to travel this distance, but the new cannon slowed the army's journey. The giant cannon was hauled by fifty oxen and 200 men on roads that needed to be paved as they went. During this long journey, the troops were ordered to attack and capture numerous towns along the coast of Marmara.

The Byzantine Empire and Constantinople were in a miserable state in 1453; no more obvious than in their dwindling population and armed forces. The Emperor had ordered a headcount of his soldiers, which consisted of 4,973 Greeks and 2,000 foreign troops. This shocking number was kept a secret by the Emperor in case it further demoralised his people. The population of the city was less than 50,000 and some estimate it could have been as low as 30,000, a number that clearly reflected the fallen power and might of the once great Byzantine Empire.

In contrast, the might of the Ottomans was seen in their numbers. Greek historians estimated 165,000 to 400,000 soldiers including 15,000 Janissaries; but some claim that the figure of 165,000 was perhaps more likely and less of an exaggeration. The troops were gathered from all corners of the Ottoman Empire. Heading towards Constantinople, Mehmed's army marched in organised and distinct rows: the Janissary archers were positioned at the centre; the azebs were on his right and left; while on the rear were the cavalry. A squadron of 350 ships sailed from Gelibolu to reach the Sea of Marmara and the Bosphorus. Never before had the Romans seen such a large fleet sail in great speed and noise towards their city.

There was a rush by Muslims to join Mehmed's army. Perhaps the main influence was the Islamic beliefs that many held dear. The famous hadiths of the Prophet Muhammad were well-known across the Ottoman Empire and men flocked to be among those honoured conquerors. In one hadith, the Prophet asked his followers,

> "Have you heard of a city with land on one side and sea on the two other sides?" They replied: "Yes, O Messenger of God." He spoke: "The last hour (of judgement) will not dawn before it is taken by 70,000 sons of Isaac. When they reach it, they will not do battle with

arms and catapults but with the words 'There is no God but Allah, and Allah is great.' Then the first sea wall will collapse, and the second time the second sea wall, and the third time the wall on the land side will collapse. And, rejoicing, they will enter it." (Sahih Muslim 2920a: Book 54, Hadith 97)

The famous walls of Constantinople today

The City of Constantinople was triangular in shape and looked like a prehistoric horn. Its famous walls reflected the marvels of human engineering and creativity and made the city invincible for centuries. Access to Constantinople through land was from the west, which was layered with double walls that ran for 19 km. The first or outer wall had a massive inaccessible trench in front of it littered with stones, while the second or inner wall was higher and sturdier. On its northern side, Constantinople sat beside the Golden Horn – a harbor linked to the Bosphorus, while its south-eastern side bordered the Sea of Marmara. Ships were always anchored on the sea sides, which was a safeguard against any potential enemy attacks. On 1453, twenty-six ships were used to defend the city. However, just before the siege, seven ships carrying 700 people were able to secretly escape Constantinople.

The Golden Horn allowed easy access from the Bosphorus to Constantinople. The Romans called it 'golden' because of the setting sun's golden reflection on its waters. To the north of this harbour was Galata, the Genoese merchant state. The Genoese did not ally themselves with anyone and were more interested in increasing their wealth and trade. They claimed that they would stay neutral in this battle but secretly, they were playing both sides. To secure the Golden Horn on April 2, 1453, the Emperor placed a heavy chain across the harbour from Constantinople to Galata, preventing ships from entering. Ironically this chain imprisoned Byzantine from the outside world and strengthened the Ottoman chokehold of their city.

On April 6, 1453, the Bosphorus and the Sea of Marmara reflected its azure blue as Byzantine soldiers took position on the famous walls of Constantinople, waiting and watching for the Ottoman troops. Across the Gate of St Romanus, leading to the Topkapı neighbourhood and beside the Golden Horn, Mehmed's troops pitched his tent, encircled by the tents of some 12,000 Janissaries. Beside his tent trenches were dug to position his giant cannon and two smaller cannons. On Mehmed's right, troops from Anatolia lined all the way from Maltape to the Sea of Marmara. On his left, the Rumelian troops took position, reaching all the way to the Golden Horn, while the reserve army was positioned behind him. His army stretched over 4 km. They wore helmets and breastplates, and carried an impressive array of weapons from shields, iron arrows, javelins, swords, and several catapults. Mehmed sent his emissaries to the emperor, calling them to *"either surrender the City or stand ready to do battle"*. The Emperor rejected this offer and Mehmed organised his generals and allocated different sites for them to attack.

Mehmed first ordered his troops to march and position themselves within 2 km from Constantinople's walls. The Emperor's mercenary knights tried to stop their advance but were pushed back inside the City walls. Meanwhile, the guns from the mighty cannons fired, weakening the forts in front of the walls. At the same time, Mehmed instructed a fleet of sixteen galleys to confront the Byzantine navy and gain access to the Golden Horn.

Siege of Constantinople, Chronique de Charles VII by Jean Chartier (illustrated circa 1470-1479).

For a week, the unrelenting fire of cannons cracked and damaged the fort's walls. However, Constantinople appeared to withstand this barrage. While the St Romanus tower had collapsed with the aid of a siege machine. However, overnight the Greeks had rebuilt the St Romanus tower and using Greek fire had burned Ottoman siege machines, proving yet again the invincibility of their city's mighty walls. Greek fire was the ancient napalm that would incinerate people and objects and could not be put out. The Byzantines had relied on Greek fire to prevent the Ottomans from easily scaling their walls. It seemed that the city walls were impenetrable but Mehmed remained undeterred and ordered for a new cannon to be built using the finest brass and bronze. Nothing could resist the force of this cannon as it would destroy a whole section of the wall.

On 12 April, a week into the siege, Mehmed ordered his fleet to attack the ships that were defending the Golden Horn. He also engineered a slightly elevated cannon. Its stones would strike the centre of galleons and immediately sink them. During this melee, three supply ships sent by the Pope sailed towards the Golden Horn. Sultan Mehmed's orders were clear – to stop them. But the Ottoman ships were smaller than the Roman ships and several Ottoman ships were sunk during the ensuing battle causing approximately 100 sailors to lose their lives and 300 were injured. Mehmed, having ridden his horse to the shore, watched it all. At first he was confident that his sailors would win and he urged them to remain steadfast but he quickly noticed the wind picking up the Italian ships' sails, opening their chance to escape. With great chagrin, he silently turned his horse and headed back.

A strong wind had pushed the Roman supply ships to sail past the Ottomans, and with the chain lowered they entered the Golden Horn. It clearly raised Byzantine morale making their emperor, Constantine XI Palaiologos, send an envoy to Mehmed calling for peace. But Sultan Mehmed rejected their offer. His teacher, Mullah Gurani, sent a letter encouraging him to continue his fight. There was also a sense of hope that the Byzantine fortification would eventually collapse. His army's morale was boosted when they noticed that the continuous bombardment of the St Romanus Gate was weakening the Byzantine ability to repair their fortifications.

Mehmed's obstacles, however, pressed on, this time in the form of his Grand vezir. During a meeting with his council of war, the Grand vezir, Halil Pasha, called an end to the siege. He argued that an annual tribute of 70,000 gold pieces from the city would be better. However, Mehmed and his close officials didn't hesitate in rejecting Halil Pasha's proposal. They were perhaps aware of the rumor that

Halil Pasha was secretly working for the Greeks and had gained much wealth for supplying them with Mehmed's plan.

It was during these frustrating delays that an ingenious idea crossed Mehmed's mind. On 22 April, the people of Constantinople awoke to a bewildering sight. Seventy Ottoman ships had crossed the steep hills of Galata and arrived at the Golden Horn. Overnight, these ships had been pulled on slipways and planks by oxen and men. The sailors had raised the sails as if they were sailing these ships on the ocean and not overland. It was an unbelievable sight that created utter panic in Byzantine who immediately transferred soldiers from other walls to face the Golden Horn, ironically weakening the overall defence of their land walls.

The following night, a Venetian captain planned to burn these Ottoman ships, but the Genoese from Galata who had pretended to be neutral secretly informed Mehmed. The Ottomans promptly sunk the Venetian ship and its thirty-three sailors were captured and executed. The Byzantines immediate revenge was to execute Ottoman prisoners on Constantinople's walls. Undeterred Mehmed ordered his troops to create a bridge to reach the city walls. The ships on the harbour were tied together using planks of wood from Genoese barrels and tied with iron hooks, allowing the soldiers to cross and reach the walls. The Byzantine failed to destroy this bridge but continued to resist and rely on their Greek fire.

A month into the siege, from sunrise to sunset the cannons continued their bombardment across numerous sites. By 16 May, Mehmed ordered tunnels to be dug, which intercepted the Byzantine tunnel and led to an underground skirmish. But he soon realised that the cannons were causing more damage and it wasn't necessary for the tunnels. His cannons had toppled both the inner wall and outer wall. Meanwhile Mehmed's navy continued to dismantle the chain across the Golden Horn but they were unsuccessful. On 18 May, the Ottomans brought a mobile wooden tower close to the city walls, but the Byzantines were successful in burning it down. Despite these drawbacks, the Ottomans continued their unrelenting attack on the city using their heavy artillery.

On 25 May, Mehmed sent his ambassador, Isfendiyar Beyoglu Ismail Bey, to offer the Byzantine Emperor the opportunity to surrender otherwise he warned them that a final assault of the city would take place. It was a generous offer as it allowed the besieged to leave with all their belongings; or if they decided to stay, they could keep their property and estate. However, the Byzantine Emperor rejected the offer.

By 26 May, they were rumours that European countries were sending a convoy of ships to support Byzantium and end the siege. Mehmed gathered his war council to consider an immediate attack. His opponents and the Grand Vezir Halil Pasha wanted to end the siege. However, Mehmed did not heed their advice and instead, turned to his confidants, Zaganos Pasha, Şerefeddin Mullah Gurani and Mullah Husrev, who encouraged him to fight on. Mehmed made a last speech urging his men to not only see the unlimited fortunes and treasures before them but to also see the honour and glory that this conquest will bestow upon them. He audaciously declared,

> *"victory is clearly on our side... be brave... silent... and mindful of the orders...I will be fighting by your side and will watch to see what each one of you do... so fight bravely and show yourself to be a hero..."*

The day before the attack, the army's silence made the Romans wary, wondering whether the Ottomans had withdrawn or to expect the worst. It was fifty days into the siege, 29 May, Mehmed awoke at dawn inspecting his troops and ordering them into battle formation. He travelled around his soldiers' camps to note their preparation and raise their morale. He reminded them to fight incessantly and give no reprieve to their enemy. There was an atmosphere of anticipation and excitement; soldiers had been promised land and high positions and those who deserted the army were promised public execution. On his horseback, Mehmed rode to all the divisions and gave specific directions to his commanders as to where, how, and when they should fight.

Meanwhile, within the Hagia Sophia church, Christians gathered in solemn prayer as their Emperor called his people to continue their defence of the city. They saw the night sky lit by Ottoman campfires, the echoes of jubilation increased their fear. The Byzantines begged God, Jesus and the Virgin Mary for help: "*Kyrie eleison! Kyrie eleison!* (*Lord have mercy!*) *Avert from us, O Lord, deliver us from the hands of our enemy!*" Their last hope, however, was a Genoese mercenary by the name of Giovanni Giustiniani-Longo.

Giustiniani was Constantinople's hero who had desperately tried to salvage the tattered walls near the St Romanus Gate which had entirely collapsed. However, he faced envy rather than support from the Byzantine officials. When Giustiniani requested that a cannon be placed before the St Romanus Gate, his request was rejected by a jealous Byzantine admiral because Giustiniani was more popular than he was. This Genoese commander's skill and efforts to defend Constantinople were further wasted when the monks, instead of using the 70,000 gold coins for building fortifications, had buried the money, which was later found by the conquering army.

On the morning of 29 May, the sun shone on the faces of the Romans blinding them to the sight of the Ottomans. The war cries of "*Allahu Akbar*" (*God is Great*) shook the grounds, announcing the Ottoman army's full-scale attack causing the Christians of Byzantine to flee and hide inside their churches. The city walls were stormed first by volunteer foot soldiers. Giustiniani knew that the attack would be on the St Romanus Gate so he positioned 3,000 men there. There was a scuffle among the Byzantine as to who should man this area and the Emperor granted Giustiniani this wish, which heightened the tension and disunity among this nobles. This also meant that other walls, watchtowers, and bastions had as few as one man to defend them.

The deafening war sound spread across the plains, with trumpets, horns, and drums, and cannons firing at the walls. All vessels were brought closer to the shores as the city was blackened by thick cannon smoke. Using ladders, bridges, wooden towers, they tried to scale the walls. It was a 'sword to sword' fight creating grave carnage. An Ottoman soldier named Hasan, raising the Ottoman flag, scaled the wall with a group of men but they all faced their death. Mehmed joined his forces and encouraged his men to fight bravely and show themselves as 'good fighters'.

The Ottomans noticed the weakening defences of the Byzantines and advanced towards the St Romanus Gate. The gate was covered with corpses, and only through the fire of the cannons an opening was made for the troops to enter the city. Mehmed called his reserve soldiers and Janissaries to join the skirmishes; for the bowmen, slingers, and musketeers to shower the walls with incessant firing and make the Byzantine troops lose all hope. He then ordered his infantry and shield bearers to cross the moat, attack the palisade and turrets and force the Byzantine to surrender.

Finally, Giovanni Giustiniani-Longo, the hero of the besieged, abandoned the Byzantine Emperor and Constantinople. He was severely wounded; an arrow had pierced his chest. He hastily left for Galata to dress his wounds and save his own life. *"My brother,"* Constantine had beseeched him to stay, *"fight bravely! Do not forsake us in our distress. The salvation of our city depends on you. Return to your post. Where are you going?"* Giustiniani's cold reply was: *"Where God himself will lead these Turks."*

Mehmed saw the fleeing Romans and could see a clear victory. He called his troops,

> *"Friends, we have the City! They are already fleeing from us! They can't stand it any longer! The wall is bare of defenders! It needs just a little more effort and the city is taken! Don't weaken... be men and I am with you!"*

When Ulubatil Hasan, a young soldier, raised the Ottoman flag on a wall, all Byzantine defences collapsed, allowing the Ottomans to enter the city from all directions. Emperor Constantine XI Palaiologos was seen on the street fighting a losing battle. His soldiers had given up. He was heard crying, "Is there no Christian here who will take my lead?" As he wailed, "the city is taken and it is useless for me to live any longer" he was struck by two *azebs* and died fighting for his city. Many of the Byzantine leaders tried to escape and some met their death before finding refuge. Prince Orhan was caught escaping and was killed.

The Byzantine populace all converged in Hagia Sophia and prayed that an angel would draw his sword drive out the Ottomans. They prayed that the Ottomans would leave Asia Minor entirely, not just Constantinople. But the Ottomans broke the doors of Hagia Sophia and imprisoned its inhabitants.

By noon, riding his horse, Sultan Mehmed entered with his Janissaries into the city of Constantinople. He first humbly prostrated to God, thanking Him for the victory. He had spent nearly two months before the walls of Constantinople and was now the Conqueror, *al-Fatih*, or *Ebu'l-Feth*, Father of the Conquest.

Upon entering Hagia Sophia, Mehmed ordered that the Muslim call to prayer (*athen*) be announced from the pulpit. It was the time for the afternoon prayers and the faithful heard, "God is the Greatest. There is no God but One God, and Muhammad is God's Prophet." Mehmed joined his congregation in prayer and Hagia Sophia now became Ayasofya mosque (*masjid*). He then climbed the dome of Ayasofya and what he saw made him reflect on the temporary nature of the world. Tursun Bey (the Ottoman historian who witnessed the conquest) wrote:

> *"The ruler of the world contemplated the marvelous works and figures inside the dome and then deigned to mount the outside of the dome. He mounted as the spirit of Jesus mounted to the fourth story of the heavens. From the galleries of the intervening stories, he viewed the sea waves of the floor and then mounted the dome. When he saw that the dependencies and outbuildings of this imposing structure lay*

in ruins, he reflected that the world is transitory and unstable and would ultimately perish."

Mehmed promised rich rewards for anyone to find the corpse of Constantine XI. At the gate of St Romanus, the Emperor's corpse lay and only his purple shoes gave away his identity. In front of Ayasofya, there was a marketplace and ceremonial square, where his severed head was displayed. A symbolic act to remind the Byzantines that they had lost and that the Ottomans were victorious.

Mehmed then ordered that the Grand Duke and admiral, Lucas Notaras, be brought to him, who was under house arrest after trying to escape. Mehmed scolded him for not surrendering and allowing the destruction to befall his city. The Duke revealed that the Emperor had received letters encouraging him to resist the siege. Finally, Mehmed found the proof he needed. He knew Halil Pasha was behind those letters and as a traitor his fate was decided. It did not take long for Halil Pasha to be imprisoned, and within forty days after the conquest he was executed. His wealth was confiscated, and his aides and friends could not mourn his death. His crime was treason by plotting and taking bribes from the Greeks. This ended the Çandarli family's hold on the post of the grand vezir. Originally the vezirs were the ulema and the first grand vezir came from the Çandarli family during the reign of Murad I. He was Kara Halil Hayreddin Çandarli who was first a judge and then became the first vezir. Halil Pasha's execution, however, paved the way for non-Turks and Christian-born converts to hold this important role.

Lucas Notaras was then freed. He was promised a role in the city's administration and 1,000 *aspers* (silver Turkish coins) was given to each of his family members. When Notaras asked Sultan Mehmed to free other officials, Mehmed agreed and even allowed them to continue their services in the new government. However, Notaras' freedom didn't last long as he and his sons were publicly executed. His enemies were jealous of the favours that he had won with Sultan Mehmed. They accused him of treason.

All the Byzantine nobles were allowed to pay for their freedom. Other Byzantine towns surrendered and the Byzantine islands paid annual tributes. The Genoese in Galata were, however, treated more fairly. Their houses were not looted and those who fled were given three months to return, otherwise their property would be seized by the state treasury. During the siege, the Genoese had promised to not support the Byzantines and in return a formal treaty had been drawn up promising the Genoese peace and security; their sons were not to be registered as Janissaries, their churches and religious practices were to be left alone but no new churches were to be built. The Ottoman troops and civilians were prohibited from entering Galata. Whilst they were permitted to elect their own leader to handle their laws and customs, they were to submit all their weaponry and accept Sultan Mehmed's order to take down their walls.

Mehmed then left Constantinople to Edrine where his scribes were ordered to dispatch letters across the Muslim world announcing his victory. His Christian neighbours came to congratulate him but were told that their taxes had increased. Venice was the first to hear of the Ottoman victory and conquest of Constantinople. It was a devastating news to the European powers, particularly to the Pope and cardinals. The Ottomans were regarded as the archenemy of Christendom and their threat was now more pronounced.

Angelo Lomellino, a nobleman from Galata, clearly saw Mehmed's imperial ambitions and wrote a warning letter to his brother in Venice:

"In sum, he has become so insolent after the capture of Constantinople that he sees himself soon becoming master of the whole world, and swears publicly that before two years have passed he intends to reach Rome, and unless the Christians take action quickly, he is likely to do things that will fill them with amazement..."

Sultan Mehmed

Hagia Sophia (Divine Wisdom), originally a site for a pagan temple, was built by Emperor Justinian I as a cathedral in 537 CE. Six years before, a smaller church on this site was burned by rioters (Nika Riots, 532 CE) who wanted to remove Justinian I from power because of his high taxes. When Justinian I saw his completed monument, he claimed, "(Prophet) Solomon, I have outdone thee." Twenty years later, its impressive dome collapsed but was restored and has remained strong for 1500 years. The Ottoman historian, Tursun Beg (15th C) exclaimed in his first sighting of this structure: "What a dome, that vies in rank with the nine spheres of heaven! In this work a perfect master has displayed the whole of the architectural science." In 1934, the secular Turkish Republic converted the Ayasofya into a museum. And for over eighty years, Muslims in Turkey tried to reclaim it as a mosque; they petitioned that Sultan Mehmed's conquest made him the Byzantine emperor and entitled him to possess all Byzantine possessions. Thus he bequeathed Ayasofya as a mosque. In 2020, Turkey's highest administrative court ruled in favour of reverting Ayasofya into a mosque.

The interior of Ayasofya

Chapter 5

BUILDING ISTANBUL

"The Seat of the Roman Empire is Constantinople and he who is and remains Emperor of the Romans is also the Emperor of the whole earth." George Trapezunitios, Greek Scholar, 15th century

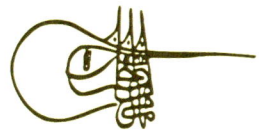

Mehmed made Constantinople the capital of the Ottoman Empire and the centre of civilisation. The Ottoman Historian Nesri considered Sultan Mehmed as the one who "created all of Istanbul." He changed the name *Konstantiniye* (Arabic for Constantinople) into *Islambol*, meaning "Islamopolis" or "City of Islam", a name preferred by his scholars. The Seljuks and the population had called it *Stinbol* or *Stambol*, later pronounced Istanbul, which was derived from Greek, *eis tēn polin*, meaning 'to the city'. Mehmed wanted Istanbul to be his capital and to restore its prestige and glory. He understood that a civilization thrived on its population, infrastructure, and education.

For the remainder of the year 1453, Mehmed gave his personal attention to building Istanbul. He ordered the repair and construction of new roads, the building of an enclosed bazaar, and the creation of numerous baths. He appointed Karistiran Suleyman Bey as the city's official governor; whose duty was to oversee the cleaning of the city, the repair of damaged walls, to appoint Muslim officials, implement Islamic law (*sharia*) and repopulate the city by calling its former inhabitants to return and resettle. People were drawn to Suleyman Bey for his intelligence and refined mannerism, making him the best person to elevate the status of this city.

Mehmed then sent an urgent decree across the Ottoman lands calling Muslims, Christians, and Jews to migrate and settle in Istanbul. He was aware that the population of Istanbul needed to grow. As an incentive he gave the Greek prisoners land along the harbours of Istanbul and ordered them to work and use their wages to gain their freedom and encouraged them to live in the city. He then personally went to Bursa to find out why the Muslims were not moving to Istanbul.

Mehmed encouraged the Christians to return to the city and allowed them to ordain their Patriarch, head of the Orthodox Church. The clergy in Istanbul elected their scholar George Scholarios Gennadius II as their Patriarch. Across Ottoman lands, Mehmed decreed that all priests and religious clergy be unharmed and excused from taxes. He stated that their churches should not be turned to mosques; that they could maintain religious independence in their marriage ceremonies and funerals, as well as any other religious rituals. They were also permitted to continue their sacred rituals at Easter. His official records reveal that approximately 50,000 Christians resettled in Istanbul.

The Jewish population also benefited from Mehmed's conquest. Jewish writers labelled Istanbul as a 'paradise' for those who desperately needed to flee persecution in Western Europe. They were given the freedom to reside in the city and continue with their trade and religious rites. Some Jews sent letters to their brethren to leave the 'torture chambers' of Europe and live under the peace and freedom of Ottoman rule. Here they were able to obtain high ranks; the personal physician of Mehmed was a Jew called Maestro Iacopo.

It was the traditional Islamic belief, clearly stated in both the Qur'an and the hadith literature, that the lives and wealth of both

Jews and Christians be safeguarded under Islamic government. Islam considers the Jews and Christians as *dhimma* or the People of the Book and the Muslims regard the Bible as a sacred text. Mehmed followed this principle and encouraged religious autonomy and tolerance. He organized a *millet* system or nations to group the different religious communities headed by their religious leader either the Greek Orthodox patriarch, the Armenian Gregorian patriarch, or the Jewish chief rabbi. This gave the different religions greater autonomy to live among the Muslims and maintain their religious identity and freedom. The Christian churches and Jewish synagogues could freely administer any legal matters related to their people excluding criminal cases. The only condition for this freedom was that they had to pay an annual *jizya*, a head tax, which gave them full protection and exempted them from conscription. However, one restriction facing these groups was that they could not sound their church bells or build new churches. Families of Greeks and Jews all successfully settled and helped create a prosperous, thriving city.

Mehmed appointed the surveyor, Tursun Beg, to record the register of the city. Tursun detailed how the empty houses were repopulated through a settlement scheme. Migrants were persuaded to resettle in rent-free accommodation. However, they were expected to pay land tax because the land was seen as *waqf*, alms to finance and support the people. This tax was donated to the soldiers who also lived in rent-free accommodation. After twenty-five years, the population had grown to eighty to one hundred thousand. And in a census in 1477, there were 14,548 houses and 3,667 shops. And in less than a century after Mehmed's death, Istanbul became one of the largest cities of the world reaching a population of four hundred thousand.

On the gate of the Grand Bazaar, *Kapalı Çarşı*, the largest covered market in the world, an Arabic calligraphy reads, *"the skill is in building a city and thus winning the hearts of the public"*. It made Mehmed's agenda clear that he was there to serve his people and make their lives easy. While the grand bazaar took gradual shape, by his death, there were 1000 or more shops. It was a rich site housing merchants from across the lands from as far as Damascus, Aleppo, and Iran.

Mehmed divided Istanbul into two distinct sections. A trading zone that housed the main bazaar where merchants from foreign lands set up shop, all working and flourishing together. And a residential zone where communities congregated around their masjid, church or synagogue. In the Top-yikgi district there were 83 households which were made up of 3 Greek, 33 Muslim and 45 Jewish residents. These districts required water supplies, which Mehmed saw as an act of charity and took personal responsibility to repair the aqueducts and built forty public fountains across Istanbul. He decreed to all able residents to construct buildings, baths and inns, markets, and masjids. His vezirs took this message and one of the outstanding masjid complex built was by Mahmud Pasha in 1462; a vezir famed for his wisdom, bravery, and many other accomplishments.

The Grand Bazaar, Kapali Çarşı

Sultan Mehmed

The maps of Florentine geographer Cristoforo Buondelmonti shows distinct architectural changes in Constantinople from 1420 to 1480. Cristoforo's map showed the notable architectural changes brought by Mehmed; his Fatih Cami, Mahmud Pasha Cami, the distinct minaret of the Hagia Sophia, palaces of Eski Saray and Topkapı, the covered Bazaar, the arsenal on the Golden Horn, and the cannon foundry on Bosphorus. Mehmed wanted to design his city according to the beliefs of Islam where the masjid became the heart of the city and its populace. Surrounding these great mosques, numerous *waqf* buildings were also established; these included soup kitchens, hospitals, and bazaars all with the intent to generate revenue and financially support the populace. These buildings became the central hub of the city where the population could easily access religious, social, and economic services. It became known as *Imaret Kulliye* or social services.

Twelve townships emerged around the *Imaret Kulliye*, these included Hagia Sophia and Fatih Kulliye. Mehmed transformed the Hagia Sophia into a great mosque, Ayasofya Cami. Its maintenance was generated through the waqf, which would annually raise 790,000-698,000 akce (50 akce was equivalent to one Venetian gold). The first great mosque that he built was dedicated to Abu Ayyub Al-Ansari, the famous companion of the Prophet who had been buried beside the wall of Constantinople. The leading scholar of his realm, Şerefeddin had a dream that guided him to the burial site of Abu Ayyub's grave. Within five years after the conquest, a large mosque was built on this site which also included a medrese, a caravanserai, public bath house, refectory and a bazaar. And the very first library in Istanbul that housed several thousand manuscripts. It became a unique *Imaret Kulliye* beyond the city walls known as Eyup district. As the population grew, it was common to see the ulama, askeri, merchants, tradesmen and craftsmen all congregated in these *imarets*, making it the heart of the city.

Map of Constantinople by Cristoforo Buondelmonti between 1420-1430

Sultan Mehmed

Map of Istanbul by Cristoforo Buondelmonti between 1485-1490

From February 1463, Mehmed focused much of his attention on building his own mosque, *The Masjid of the Conqueror,* or in Arabic, *Fatih Cami*. In the summer of 1471, it was open to the public, eight years after construction had begun. It showcased a unique Ottoman architectural design distinct from the engineering style of the Byzantine Empire. *Fatih Cami* was built in the middle of a park, a rectangular building, making its courtyard quite popular. Its twenty-two domes were anchored by eight granite and marble columns. The inside of this *masjid* had numerous windows which filled it with natural light, making it incomparable to the masjids of the 1400s. Upon entering the *masjid,* a marble tablet with golden Arabic calligraphy engraved the Prophet Muhammad's Hadith: *"Verily you shall conquer Constantinople. What a wonderful leader will her leader be, and what a wonderful army will that army be!"*

The Masjid of the Conqueror, Fatih Cami, built in 1471

Numerous charitable buildings were constructed around

Mehmed's masjid. These included: eight *medreses* (schools) each with 19 rooms and dormitories, a hospital, an almshouse, kitchens and *hamam* (bathhouse), a building for travellers, guest houses, a library, a primary school (*mektep*), gardens, and water wells. Around 102 people worked in Fatih Cami, 168 in the medrese and 30 in the hospital. All subjects were given great importance particularly the Qur'an as well as other subjects such as mathematics, philosophy, logic, and Islamic theology, something that Mehmed personally encouraged. The eight *medreses* ran ten courses which comprised of language, philosophy, public speaking, mathematics, astronomy, and four theological courses including beliefs, *Sharia*, hadith, and *Tafseer* (exegesis of the Qur'an). Upon graduation, the students would receive a certificate that called them a *danismend* – one who has mastery of the discipline and could teach. The school attached to the *masjid* was by far one of the most prestigious schools in all of the Ottoman Empire and was labelled as the 'paradise of learning'. Mehmed used his Cami to promote and enshrine a culture of learning across his Empire and his appreciation of learning was reflected in his patronage of numerous *medreses* across the Empire, catering to different levels and skills.

A gate leading to Fatih Cami

Mehmed was always in the company of scholars, earning him the title of 'patron of science and learning.' Often, he would discuss philosophical works of Arabs, Persians, and Greeks particularly Peripatetics and Stoics. He invited the famed scholar Hocazade of Bursa (d. 1488) to review the theological and philosophical works of al-Ghazali and Ibn Rushd. In this study, Hocazade argued that sharia is to be defended against philosophy and that while reason suffices in mathematics it is, however, limited in the realm of theology. Mehmed also enjoyed literature and supported thirty poets and scholars. Under his pseudonym Avni, he dabbled in composing eighty Turkish poems, his work is titled *Divan*, expressing his love for the Prophet Muhammad. It was a tradition then to have the Prophet as the subject of one's poetry.

Mehmed was never far from his *medreses*, often visiting the classrooms to see for himself how great these scholars were in their expertise and pedagogy. He also gave special attention to their welfare and growth. He kept a list of the scholars' academic strengths and weaknesses and used it to appoint them according to their strengths, from basic to advanced positions. On one occasion, a scholar tried to persuade Mehmed to gift him with 124,000 *akçe* in the name of 124,000 prophets. "Very well," Mehmed had mockingly replied, "name them! I will give you one *akçe* for each one." Unfortunately, the scholar could only recall ten out of the twenty-five prophets that had been named in the Qur'an and so Mehmed gave him ten *akçe* and removed him from his post. To ensure the prestige of learning among his subjects Mehmed made sure that teachers were paid high wages. Those who taught at the 'paradise of learning' received fifty to sixty *akçe* per day. The teachers' wages reflected their rank and the subjects that they taught. The grand vezir was entrusted with the responsibility of managing the rank of the scholars (*ülema*) according to their knowledge and expertise in Islamic law and theology. One famed mathematician honoured and sponsored by Mehmed was Ali Kuscu (d. 1474), who wrote classical texts on arithmetic and astronomy and trained later mathematicians.

The interior of Fatih Cami.

The building of *Topkapı Sarayı*, the Palace of the Cannon Gate begun in 1465; it was the second palace built in Istanbul after Eski Saray and was also called the New Palace. It was situated on a hilltop facing the Sea of Marmara and the Golden Horn. It had once been the acropolis of the Romans. Mehmed employed the Persian architect Kemaleddin to create a unique look by using faience (glazed non-clay ceramic) to make blue-green tiles as well as colonnades. Topkapı Palace was divided into three courtyards separated by 3 m high walls with sturdy defence towers. Numerous buildings encircled each court with separate quarters for men and women as well as halls, porticoes, bakeshops, and baths. The courtyards had lush gardens with fruit trees, vineyards, array of flowers including roses, lilacs, saffron, and even housed a zoology and an aviary. The stream of fountains and pools added to the serene atmosphere. By 1479, Mehmed had completed its construction.

A library inside the Topkapı Palace.

Through the Imperial Gate (*Bab-i Hümayun*) visitors and government servants entered this majestic palace, showcasing Mehmed's distinct contribution and patronage of architecture. *Bab-i Hümayun* allowed the public to enter the First Court and access the varied service buildings such as a hospital, kitchen, arsenal, and treasury. It was also the court of the Janissaries. The *Bab-es Selam* or Gate of Peace, had a waiting room for ambassadors and opened to the Second Court. It housed the Divan, Mehmed's Imperial Council.

Selim III receiving dignitaries at an audience in front of the Gate of Peace, image from Topkapı Museum archives

The Divan met four times a week to discuss and administer official matters. This court would be filled with 5000 officials and on special occasions 10,000. The Venetian ambassador witnessed this and recounted in awe:

> "I entered into the court, where I found on one side all the Janissaries on foot, and on the other side all of the persons of high esteem, and the salaried officials of His Majesty, who stood with such great silence and with such a beautiful order, that it was a marvelous thing, not believable to one who has not seen it with his own eyes."

The Third Court housed the Palace School which trained select individuals for Imperial service. Many pashas and distinguished officials graduated from this school. Later sultans developed Topkapı extensively, making it an official Ottoman Court during the 16th

Century. It came to house approximately 40,000 people and gained the famous nickname 'a city within a city.'

Mehmed had turned Istanbul into a thriving city, but the emergence of a devastating plague held him perplexed and powerless. The Black Death took its menacing toll upon Europe and Asia and by 1469, the plague had devastated the population of Istanbul and other European cities such as Florence. It drastically reduced the population of Bursa. People were dying at the rate of 600 burials per day. Some lay dead within their houses for days. There were few grave diggers, and the city was nearly deserted. Mehmed avoided his capital and sought refuge in the mountains of Bulgaria where no one was allowed to approach; they were ordered to stay a day's distance. This practice of isolation during a plague was taught by Prophet Muhammad. In one hadith, he had emphasised that one should avoid the city that has a plague by not entering it or leaving it to ensure that it does not spread.

Whilst in the Balkan Mountains, Mehmed encouraged his court to find medical remedies. Mahmud Pasha's letter addressed to the Republic of Dubrovnik showed Mehmed's interest in medicine and the importance that he gave it. It requested medical manuscripts as well as the Latin commentaries on Ibn Sina's *Kanin fi't-tibb* (Cannon of Medicine), which would obviously support his physician's research. This knowledge was carried to his hospital beside his mosque, Fatih Cami. His hospital included two doctors, an eye specialist, a surgeon and a pharmacist. It helped anyone and accepted people who could not pay for their treatment or buy the medicine. This hospital was later developed to also include a separate hospital for women. The hospital's expenses were met through the waqf.

During this dire health crisis, a growing trade link emerged between the Ottomans and the Florentines. Despite the hostility from Italians and other Ottoman foes, the Florentines turned to the Ottomans for mutual trade benefits. Mehmed was very much aware that friendly trade links were an important means to enrich Istanbul. For this reason, he gave special trading opportunities to the Florentines whose leaders expressed "undying gratitude" and considered Sultan Mehmed a "benefactor".

Before the plague had hit, Mehmed turned to his greatest passion, geography. Clearly it was linked to his thirst for conquest. Among his library of 8,000 manuscripts of multiple languages, he paid particular attention to Ptolemy's world map, *Geographia*. Ptolemy was an Egyptian astronomer and geographer during the 2nd century CE. Mehmed decided that it was not enough to get a clear picture of the known world from fragmentary maps, so he ordered that all these partial maps be assembled as one, known as *mappa mundi*. This was a laborious task, but it was one that the Conqueror wished to see. In 1465, he appointed the cousin of Mahmud Pasha, George Amirutzes of Trebizond, to create a wall map that would show him the extend of the Ottoman empire across the inhabited world. This map became the source of Islamic and later Renaissance cartography.

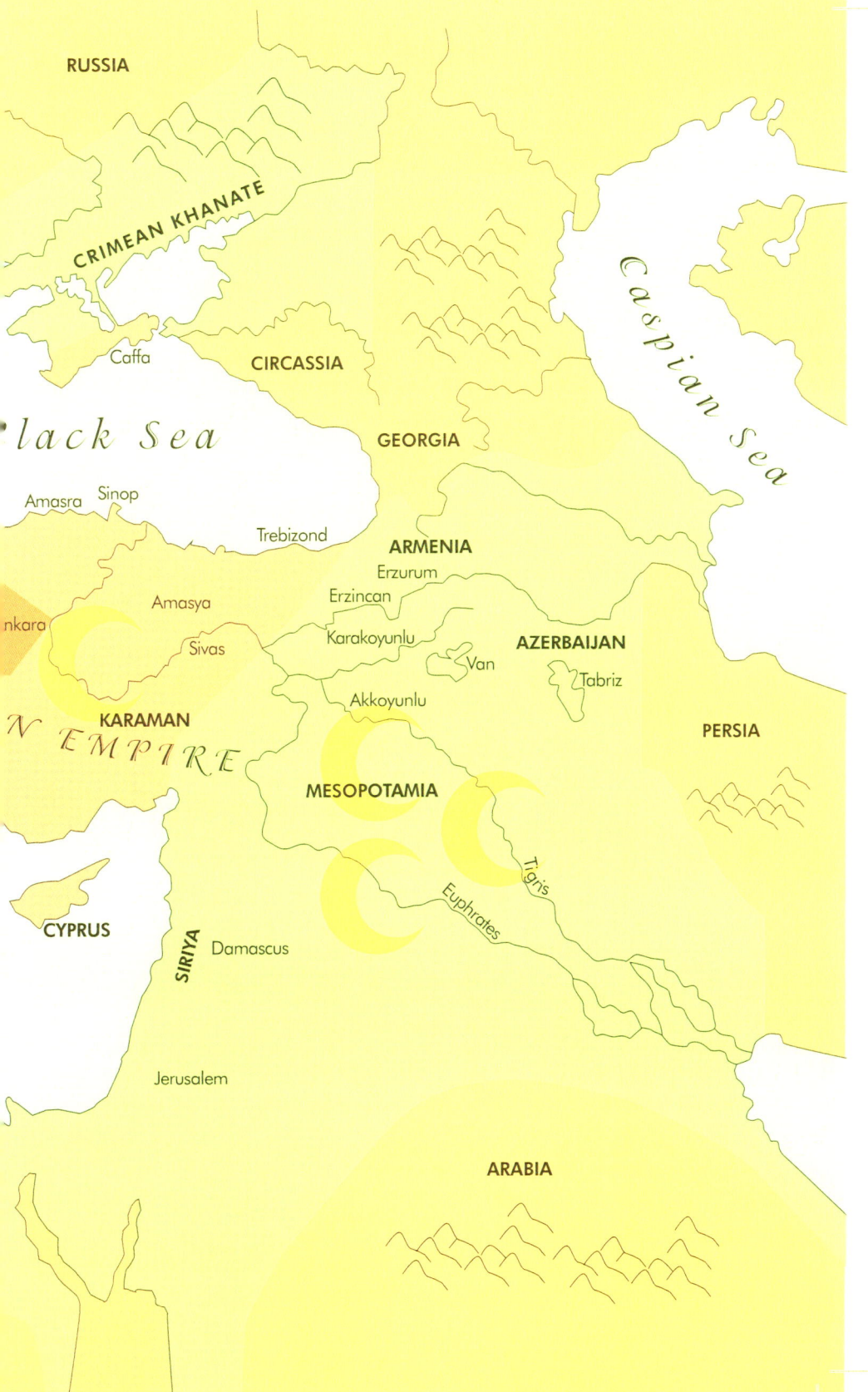

Chapter 6

OTHER CONQUESTS

"If the hair of my beard knew my plans, I would pull it out and burn it." Sultan Mehmed II

The conquest of Constantinople did not quench Mehmed's ambitions. He was driven to outdo his predecessors, whether they were Ottoman rulers or leaders such as Alexander the Great or Julius Caesar. His life goal was to establish: "one faith, one Empire, and one rule."

Mehmed spent most of his time acquiring knowledge of his neighbours, particularly the Western world, its kingdoms, battles, and weaponry. He employed Romans to help him understand Rome and kept a detailed map of Italy and Europe with clear indications of their geography. As a consequence, the Italians were most worried about the Ottoman expansion.

For a year after the conquest, Mehmed did not seek the aid of a vezir to rule; he was the sole sovereign. Once he decided to choose a vezir, he continued to retain the role of president over the crown council and on occasion had the grand vezir head the army. The crown council was called the *divan*. It held meetings from Saturday to Tuesday to discuss matters relevant to the Empire but also hear complaints from anyone. It acted as a high court to which Mehmed presided over and was never absent from. The purpose of this council was to establish justice and security in the realms.

The Divan, Mehmed's Imperial Council meeting hall, Topkapı Palace

Gradually Mehmed increased the number of vezirs from three to four. The first vezir had a range of official powers: he was recognised as the Sultan's representative and his head of administration carrying out executive orders. He held the imperial seal that opened the treasury locks, had special marshals to escort and guard him and many ceremonial privileges. Mehmed described the role of the grand vezir as:

"The head of the vezirs and commanders. He is greater than all men; he is in all matters the sultan's absolute deputy."

After Halil Pasha's dramatic execution, the honoured role of grand vezir was bestowed upon Zaganos Mehmed Pasha who was

Mehmed's childhood confidant and whose daughter he had married. He was then replaced with Mahmud Pasha Angelovic, who was a Serbian convert to Islam. When Mahmud Pasha lost favour, he was replaced by another convert, Rum Mehmed Pasha, who was later replaced by Gedik Ahmed Pasha. While political rivalry may have played a role in the dismissal of his vezirs, however, Mehmed was also an astute leader who was ever watchful of his vezirs' conduct and had high expectations of them.

After the conquest of Constantinople, the European powers were left scrambling to find ways to save themselves and prevent Ottoman advance upon their territories. Venice had rushed to negotiate a peace treaty with Sultan Mehmed, and later apologised to the Pope for doing so. Some kings, such as Alfonso of Naples, made big claims about launching a crusade but had no intention of doing so. Other European powers such as England, Germany and France were also not in favour of launching a crusade. It was their silence that greeted the Catholic Church's urgent call-to-arms.

A bishop wrote a letter to Pope Nichola V, urging him to launch a crusade against Mehmed:

> *"Already the sword of the Turks hovers over our heads; already the Black Sea is closed to us; already Wallachia is in the hands of the Turks. Thence they will invade Hungary and then Germany. Meanwhile we live in discord and enmity. The kings of England and France have taken arms against each other. Seldom is all Spain at peace and the Italian states can never find peace in their struggle for hegemony. How much better it would be if we were to turn our weapons against the enemies of our faith!"*

The Pope responded by sending a message in 1454, calling for an urgent crusade, yet it failed to bring together the European leaders. There were rumours that the Pope himself, along with other kings, were motivated by filling their pockets more than anything else.

Serbia

In 1455, Mehmed decided to launch another attack on his Western enemies. Isa Bey, who ruled southern Serbia, encouraged him to consider conquering all of Serbian territory because they were colluding with the Hungarians. Mehmed's first campaign after the conquest of Constantinople was Serbia primarily to access its rich silver mines and use this to strengthen his army.

With his battalion, Isa Bey reached the walls of the Serbian city, Novo Brdo. He demanded their surrender and when they refused, Mehmed personally arrived with 50,000 horsemen. The siege lasted for forty days and nights. On 1 June, 1455, Novo Brdo surrendered. It was an important city in the Balkans, called the 'mother of cities' as it was a commercial hub with numerous gold and silver mines. The residents signed a treaty in which Mehmed promised them continued residence and security in their businesses, particularly those who were miners. However, the officials of Novo Brdo were sentenced to death and approximately 320 men were sent to the Janissary corps.

During this campaign, Mehmed learned that the Hungarians were preparing to launch an attack. He could not continue his campaign against Serbia because his immediate attention was needed in Greece and dealing with Hungarian attacks. However, four years later, in 1459, his army returned and successfully captured the Serbian capital, Smederova, causing the rest of Serbia to surrender.

* * *

Aegean Islands

The Ottoman navy became a powerful force after the fall of Constantinople as Mehmed wanted to outdo the Venetian and Genoese navies. His aim wasn't just to conquer land but also to control the seas. The largest Greek island, Rhodes, confidently refused to give an annual tribute, which gave Mehmed an easy excuse to use his navy against them. The crusader Knights of Saint John had occupied Rhodes since 1310. They argued that it belonged to the Pope who did not pay tribute to even western kings. They promised instead to give annual gifts to Sultan Mehmed.

Mehmed send an impressive fleet to devastate the island of Rhodes. On the coast of Gelibolu around 25 triremes, 50 biremes and 100 small vessels (triremes had three rows of oarsman while biremes had two) sailed. Hamza Bey, the admiral of the fleet, was instructed to head over to the Greek island of Chios before attacking Rhodes to collect a debt that Chios owed Mehmed's friend, Francesco Draperio, which amounted to 40,000 ducats (Venetian gold coins). But although the Chios paid annual tributes to the Sultan, they refused to pay their debt to Draperio.

Despite being successful in land attacks, Admiral Hamza could not wage a proper sea attack. His ships lacked enough weaponry and manpower. He was forced to abandon Chios and could not see a possible attack on Rhodes being successful. However, on the way to Gelibolu, he passed Chios again in the hope of claiming the debt. But the inhabitants of Chios showed hostility and sunk his best vessel. Mehmed was infuriated by Hamza Bey and removed him from his post. Mehmed welcomed Draperio in his palace and said to him,

> *"You now owe me forty thousand. I forgive you the debt, but I am taking over your claim against the people of Chios, who are to pay me double the amount and an indemnity for the Turkish blood they have shed."*

Sultan Mehmed's navy continued to grow despite Hamza Bey's removal and the lack of success over Chios and Rhodes. In 1455, a new admiral, Yunus Bey, was appointed. He was given charge of ten trireme and numerous biremes anchored on the coast of Gelibolu. Yunus Bey was a Spaniard of Catalan origin. His first mission was to reclaim the loss against Chios, but unfortunately, his voyage faced a storm that sank twenty vessels. His fleet was nearly all but destroyed and he had no hope of fighting. Yunus Bey too retreated but on his way back he destroyed many Chios merchant ships, took prisoners and brought spoils to Sultan Mehmed. Complaints by the Greeks against Yunus Bey was ignored by Mehmed.

It was not not long into his reign that a simple threat from Mehmed would cause capitulation in the Aegean islands. Sultan Mehmed ordered the capture of Eski Foca, a harbour town located north-east of Chios. Its Duke, however, surrendered without any resistance. This became the pattern for most Aegean islands and coastal towns, as one-after-another, they were taken over by Mehmed's fleet without the need for using any force.

On the northern shores of the Aegean Sea, Enez was a popular coastal town that Mehmed showed interest in. It was famous for its rich wildlife and salt-panning industry, earning the island 300,000 silver annually. After the death of its ruler, there was a struggle for power between his widow and her brother-in-law. The widow, however, sent messengers to the Ottoman court to allege that her brother-in-law was plotting to overthrow Ottoman sovereignty. Enez was an Ottoman vassal and was expected to give annual tax, however, its ruler refused and was also secretly helping pirates to attack Muslim villages and plotting with the Italians.

Mehmed did not need an excuse to launch an attack and possess Enez. He marched with his army across a frozen landscape that caused frostbite to many soldiers, whilst his admiral, Yunus Bey, brought ten triremes to block the sea access to Enez. It was January 1456 and unfortunately for the people of Enez, their ruler had left their city to escape the bitter cold. They had no choice but to surrender and plea for security and safety. Mehmed accepted their surrender and easily possessed their ruler's treasures of gold and silver.

* * *

On the way to Hungary

After the campaign in Serbia, Sultan Mehmed gave his troops some respite, even though he was itching to launch an expedition against Hungary. The route to Hungary was through Serbia and Mehmed had virtually subjugated most of Serbia by 1455. To reach the rest of Europe, Mehmed needed to remove Hungary especially because all the treaties with them had a history of being fragile and easily broken.

Before launching his offensive on Hungary, Mehmed turned his attention to Moldavia (Romania) located north-west of the Black Sea. He sent the prince a letter demanding an annual tribute of 2,000 gold to guarantee Moldavia's security and peace, which the Moldavian prince accepted. The letter read:

> *"From the great sovereign and great Emir Sultan Mehmed Bey to the noble, wise and estimable Iona Petru, Voivode and Lord of Mavrovlachia. Receive friendly greetings, Your Excellency. You have sent your emissary, the boyar Mahalia the Logothete. And My Highness has taken note of all the words he has said. If you send My Highness Harac (head tax) in the amount of 2,000 gold ducats each year, let there be perfect peace. And I grant you a delay of three months. If [the head tax] arrives within this time, let there be complete peace with my highness. But if it does not arrive, you know [what will happen]. And let God rejoice you! On the fifth day of October, in Sarukhanbeyli!"*

Mehmed's order, *firman,* guaranteed the Moldavians peace and the right to trade without facing hostility in the Ottoman territories.

After easily subjugating Moldavia, Mehmed then faced the Hungarians. To the south of Moldavia was Wallachia, which had no serious army that could stop the Ottoman advance toward Hungary. However, the key to the capture of Hungary was the Serbian city, Belgrade. Mahmed needed to make Belgrade into an Ottoman military base where attacks on Hungarian territories could be launched.

He famously said that once Belgrade fell, it would take him two months to eat his dinner in Buda, the capital of Hungary.

An estimated 150,000 to 400,000 troops were prepared for attack, stationed between Istanbul and Edirne. He ordered his army to approach from both sea and land. A massive fleet sailed, consisting of 200 light vessels and larger ships carrying ammunition such as cannons. Workers set up shop to supply Mehmed's new cannons with mortars and cannon balls. Despite all efforts to keep the campaign secret, the Hungarians were well aware of the impending attack.

Belgrade was impenetrable, fortified on all sides with two raging rivers and steep banks and double walls with deep moats. And its army was well equiped and ready for battle. On 13 June 1456, Mehmed and his troops arrived and stationed his tent in the vicinity of Belgrade. His Janissaries lined the horizon. There were 300 siege guns, 27 heavy cannons and seven mortars facing the fortress of Belgrade. Mehmed also placed several ships tied with chains to prevent access and passage across the Danube, the main river that ran through Belgrade.

Meanwhile, the Hungarian King, Ladislas V, had escaped Buda in the dead of night to the safety of Vienna. It was only John Hunyadi, the Hungarian general, who gathered some 60,000 troops to face the ominous Ottomans. However, his troops were poorly equipped with a worthless number of vessels because the European leaders had remained silent and didn't support him.

Mehmed's cannons mercilessly bombarded the fortress of Belgrade throughout the day and night. The inhabitants saw the hurling boulders and took flight. When Hunyadi's fleet reached the Danube, he was able to destroy the Ottoman galleys and break through the chained ships. A fierce fight ensued turning the Danube the colour of blood. Approximately 500 Ottoman sailors drowned and Sultan Mehmed ordered that no vessel was to be taken by his enemies but burned in the sea instead. Hunyadi's success in the Danube helped his army enter the fortress of Belgrade. While the besieged continued to repair their defences, the Ottoman cannons did not cease their unrelenting barrage.

A week after the crushing defeat in the Danube, Mehmed ordered his troops to launch a full-scale attack on Belgrade. It was a battle that lasted through the night. By dawn, the Janissaries managed to scale the walls and enter the fortress. Upon entry, they saw few troops and thought that they had achieved victory. However, they were ambushed. In a surprise attack, countless Janissaries were massacred by Hunyadi's troops who were hiding and waiting. His troops dipped bundles of twigs in sulphur and threw the lit bundles onto the groups of Janissaries who had been waiting in ditches to launch their attack. This devastated the Ottoman attack and created a horrible scene of burned corpses as far as the eye could see. Hunyadi's battle tactic boosted his troops' morale and they advanced upon the Ottoman lines, which they captured one by one, until they reached the tent of Mehmed. Mehmed's vezir's advised him to retreat and his response was, *"To turn one's face from the enemy is the sign of defeat. Allah has granted high fortune to me."* He then fearlessly threw himself into the battle until he was seriously injured with an arrow in his thigh.

The Ottoman losses were great and Mehmed wisely called his troops to retreat but he made sure that Ottoman weaponry would be burned and not become spoils for the enemy. In the Hungarian camp there was an excited rumour that Sultan Mehmed had died and that even Constantinople had been recaptured.

Encouraged by his win, John Hunyadi sent a letter to the Pope urging him to send 10,000 well-equipped horsemen to further the crusader campaign and use this as an opportunity to be rid of the Ottoman Empire once and for all. He believed that this defeat had crushed Sultan Mehmed and his army. In their enthusiasm, his army launched a sea campaign to gain control of the Aegean and its many islands. In 1456, 1,000 seamen, 5,000 soldiers and 300 guns were brought to the Aegean. The Pope had spent 150,000 ducats, roughly equivalent to 22 million dollars today. However, this crusade came with countless problems. Firstly, the sixteen vessels were too few in number for the size of the campaign and the leaders of the expedition were too busy squandering the money on themselves and paying their debts. No leader took the initiative to finance the campaign except for the Pope whose resources and finances were dwindling.

Then in 1456, Hunyadi, the only leader who was personally motivated by the crusading cause, died unexpectedly when the bubonic plague swept southeastern Europe. And the discord among European leaders continued with executions, prison sentences and jostling for power. George Brankovic, the King of Serbia, also died and his son, Lazar, who succeeded him, signed a treaty with the Ottoman Empire to pay an annual tribute of 20,000 ducats (equivalent to 3 million dollars). This was an easy decision on behalf of the Serbians who were not on friendly terms with their neighbours, the Hungarians.

After Hunyadi's death, Mehmed's main opponent was George Castriota Skanderbeg, the prince of Albania. Skanderbeg had been raised in the Ottoman court but left it to return and serve his people in Albania, becoming their legendary hero. During the battle of Belgrade, Ottoman forces were sent to divert Skanderbeg and force him north. During these battles in Albania, some sources claim that Skanderbeg massacred thousands of Ottoman soldiers, perhaps up to 30,000. He found his nephew among the troops and discovered he had converted to Islam. He took him prisoner for treason and apostasy against the church.

However, by 1457, Skanderbeg faced grave financial difficulties as there were little funds to properly equip his soldiers against the Ottoman power. Even the Pope was unable to meet the enormous resources required. The most that Skanderbeg achieved was to unify the Albanian chiefs against any possible threat posed by the Ottomans.

After his defeat at Belgrade, Mehmed spent 1457 in Edirne. He didn't participate in any battles either, perhaps because of his injury. He was seemly occupied with celebrating his two sons' circumcisions and sent invitation letters across the known Eastern kingdoms, even to the Doge Francesco Foscari of Venice. This letter has been preserved and reads:

> "The great lord and grand emir Sultan Mehmed Bey. To the most excellent, most glorious, most noble, most prudent, most powerful, most praiseworthy and honourable; to our dearly beloved and revered father, Doge of the most illustrious Signoria of Venice. May your Grace and his counselors as well receive fit, proper, and honourable greeting from My Magnificence. We wish to call it to your grace's attention that with God's help we are planning to celebrate the circumcision of Our sons. And by the peace and friendship that we observe with your Grace! And since we are informed by Our slaves here present that you harbor the same affection for us, we send hereby Our slave Kara Hasan to invite you to our rejoicing, according to our tradition. On the seventeenth day of March, 1457."

The circumcisions of Bayezid and Mustafa was celebrated for four days in the Edirne palace. It was a gathering that included renowned scholars who recited and explained verses from the Qur'an. During the first day, Mehmed viewed the grand recitals from his throne. On either side of him sat esteemed religious scholars. On the second day, the poor were invited and given a lavish reception with food and entertainment such as storytelling and poetry recitals. On the third day, the Ottoman nobility were entertained with horse races and archery challenges. The fourth day concluded the ceremonies with Mehmed giving gifts of money to his people but also receiving gifts from his dignitaries and officials.

Greece

The disaster at Belgrade did not stop Mehmed's campaigns; instead, he turned his attention to Greece. When the Greek towns of Mistra and Patras failed to pay their overdue tributes of three years, Mehmed sent them the following letter:

> *"How could you voluntarily promise an annual tribute of 10,000 gold pieces when I now see that you despise me and concern yourselves not at all with the treaties that were concluded? Now, of two things choose the one which seems better to you: either pay the tribute that is due, and then let peace prevail between us, or go away quickly and leave your country to my rule!"*

In April 1458, Mehmed led his army to conquer Greece. Unfortunately for the Greeks, they lacked the leadership to organise themselves and resist the Ottoman advance. Just before he laid siege, a tribute was brought by Greek nobles, but it was too little and too late. Mehmed scornfully replied that he would decide on a treaty once he arrived in Morea, the Peloponnese peninsula in southern Greece.

Located in south-central Greece, Corinth was situated on the summit of a hill and had triple walls. Mehmed brought his whole army for the siege of Corinth and the residents were given the chance to peacefully surrender. This was an Islamic tradition which Mehmed honoured, promising the inhabitants of Corinth safety and security to reside in any Ottoman territory. However, the ruler of Corinth refused to surrender peacefully and was confident that his walls would defeat the Ottomans. The Ottomans could not scale the steep walls and faced the barrage of Corinthian long spears, javelins, axes and stones hurled at them.

Mehmed's response was to use every means he had to bring the city to its knees. He brought his heavy guns, the cannons that were made of marble from Ancient Greek temples. The plan was to hit with these projectiles that weighed hundreds of kilograms, however, it was difficult for Mehmed's cannons to effectively hit and damage these walls. While at first Mehmed relied on his cannons to do the job because it was impossible to scale the defensive walls of Corinth. He then ordered his troops to bring approximately 150,000 supplies of sheep, oxen and horses and starve the city into submission. Eventually the ceaseless bombardment and the shortage of supplies made the besieged turn to Mehmed, giving him an advantage over the treaty terms. He demanded all surrounding cities to be handed over to him with an additional annual tribute of 3,000 gold pieces.

Meanwhile, Mahmud Pasha was sent to the interior of the Peloponnese and in the same manner, many Greek towns and cities were besieged and either mercilessly conquered or surrendered out of desperation. These included Tarsos, Phlius, Akribe, Rupela and Muchli. The Ottomans made sure that the siege always ended in their favour, whether through denying the besieged access to water or blocking their escape routes. The historian George Sphrantzes (d. 1478) wrote that the Greeks surrendered their lands *"like garden vegetables"*. In total, 250 Greek towns were taken by Mehmed. And the Ottoman Janissaries took immediate post within these towns.

It was only five years after gaining his prestigious title, the Conqueror, that Mehmed in 1458 successfully conquered Athens, the heart of the ancient Western civilisation. It remained under Turkish rule for the next 330 years. On entering this ancient city, Mehmed marvelled at its historic beauty, especially the sight of the Acropolis, the citadel in Athens that held the Parthenon, the Ancient Greek temple. He appreciated its beauty as the *"city of philosophers"* and was generous to its inhabitants by exempting them from the head tax and devşirme as well as ordering religious tolerance to the Orthodox Christians. Mehmed only stayed in Athens for a mere four days. He donated funds for a small mosque to be built in the Roman agora, named Fatih Cami, which is still standing. He then left Athens and visited other conquests such as Thebes.

Near the city of Athens was one of the largest Greek islands, Negroponte. It was under Venetian rule and in treaty with the

Ottomans. Out of curiosity, and perhaps with the intent to one day conquering it, Mehmed requested to enter the city with his army. The Venetians regarded Negroponte as their commercial jewel in the Aegean Sea. Their reaction to Mehmed's request was obvious fear, but he promised them no harm and that he simply wanted to see their "commercial jewel". He crossed the bridge that connected Negroponte to mainland Greece with a thousand horsemen and viewed the city from its highest hill. Twelve years later he did return as its conqueror.

The year 1459 marked two victories for Mehmed; both Greece and the entire Serbian territory came under his rule. When he arrived on the borders of the famed Serbian city of Smederevo, he met no resistance because the nobles flung their city gates open giving Mehmed its keys.

The year also ended with another special occasion for Mehmed to celebrate. On 22 December 1459, his third son was born. He was named Cem, and he became an adventurous prince who met a tragic death by poisoning in 1495. There were also rumours as to his mother's identity; whether she was Serbian or a Turkish Muslim.

*　*　*

The Pope's call for a Crusade

In 1458, a new pope assumed his position at the Vatican, Pope Pius II, and his main objective was to be rid of the Turks once and for all. However, all his efforts to unify the Christian leaders failed and he was unsuccessful in bringing about a crusade against the Muslims. In a two-hour long speech, he pleaded with the European kings and princes to fight the Ottomans:

> "We ourselves allowed Constantinople... to be conquered by the Turks. And while we sit at home in ease and idleness, the arms of these barbarians are advancing to the Danube and the Sava... they

have massacred the successor of Constantine along with his people, desecrated the temples of the Lord... for Mehmed will never lay down arms except in victory... Every victory will be for him a stepping-stone to another..."

His desperate appeals fell upon deaf ears. The Western kings and princes were too busy squabbling about who should provide more resources to equip the crusades. The Venetians were particularly demanding; they asked for total command of the fleet and to be the first to take the spoils. While they had the most wealth to give, they demanded more manpower from their neighbouring countries. All their plans and promises were without any serious or honest commitment.

Pope Pius II then came up with the idea of converting Sultan Mehmed to Christianity. He wrote him a letter, which was never sent and even if it had been, it would have been difficult to convert Mehmed to Christianity. The letter read:

" ...a little water with which to be baptised, to be converted to Christianity... Once you have done this there will be no prince on the whole earth to outdo you in fame or equal you in power. We shall appoint you emperor of the Greeks and the Orient... All Christians will honour you and make you arbiter of their quarrels..."

Meanwhile, Mehmed's Italian spies kept him well informed of the crusader plans and their failure to launch a crusade. Speaking to a Florentine chronicler and merchant, Benedetto Dei, Mehmed confidently expressed why the Italians and the crusaders were failing to challenge him:

"My Florentine, I have heard all you have said...and I believe it fully...Italy could no longer perform the great deeds it performed in the past... the Romans, who were then sole masters of Italy...but today you are twenty states ... and you are bitter enemies... and seeing that I

am young and rich and favoured by fortune, I intend to surpass Caesar and Alexander and Xerxes by far."

The different Italian states were struggling to challenge Ottoman authority. The Genoese in particular could no longer trade easily through the Black Sea because of the presence of the Rumali Hisari. They sought to regain Galata, but Sultan Mehmed reminded them that it was acquired through friendly agreements. In 1460, Mehmed sent his grand vezir, Mahmud Pasha, to end their power in the city of Amasra and their commercial hopes in the Black Sea. It was an easy task to capture Amasra, located on the southern shores of the Black Sea. The inhabitants surrendered without any resistance and two-thirds of its population were taken to Istanbul.

* * *

Trebizond

In 1461, Mehmed led a massive army up north to the Black Sea. No one knew of his plans. When anyone dared to ask, his reply was,

"If the hair of my beard knew my plans, I would pull it out and burn it."

He ordered 300 vessels to be led by Admiral Kashmir Pasha. It included triremes, fifty oared vessels, armoured and supply ships. The freights carried cannons and an array of shields, helmets, spears, breastplates, different sizes of arrows, bows and crossbows. Mehmed organised 60,000 cavalry and 80,000 infantry to cross Anatolia. These troops were from Rumelia (Europe) and as the army crossed the Bosphorus strait to Anatolia, the number of soldiers increased.

The city of Sinop was on Mehmed's route and in it Ibrahim Bey, his brother-in-law, had sought refuge. Mehmed asked the *divan* secretary, Tursun Beg to send a message to Ismail Bey to surrender the city, and Ismail Bey readily accepted the offer:

> "You are now surrounded by land and sea. There is no choice of escape. You ought to think of your own and your family's honour. Your people have not yet fallen prey to the army. Take pity on them and surrender your fortresses and your lands. In return the Sultan will give you other lands to administer, and you will live a life of ease under his protection. In the event that you do not surrender, remember that there is nothing that can stop our soldiers. Consider this admonition as a sign of our friendship."

The route Mehmed followed was rough and treacherous. His troops travelled for 14 days across deep ravines and steep mountains. Yet they marched in formation and only changing to suit the terrain. The infantry were in the wings, the supplies in the centre, and the cavalry at the back. It was a perfect order, even the right handed bowmen were stationed on the left and left handed bowman were on the right and the spearmen carried their spears ready for battle.

Mehmed's march gave the impression that he was on a campaign to conquer Uzun Hasan's possessions, and not the city of Trebizond. Uzun Hasan was the ruler of the White Sheep Turkoman (Akkoyunlu), a tribe of the Oghuz Turks who had control over eastern Anatolia and parts of modern Iraq, Azerbaijan, Iran, Transcaucasia and Syria. Uzan Hasan was often collaborating with Trebizond to undermine Ottoman rule. Trebizond was one of the last remnants of the Eastern Roman Empire; it was a famed ancient Greek city located in the north-eastern Anatolia on the shores of the Black Sea. It was also famous for its prosperous trade links to Asia and its rich agriculture.

Before reaching his destination, he was met with Sara Hatun, who sought a peaceful treaty on behalf of her son, Uzun Hasan. Mehmed was very generous and concluded a peace treaty with Hasan, with the clear condition that Hasan would not support the Comneni (or Komnenos), the Byzantine family who ruled Trebizond.

Sara Hatun's pleas for the protection of Trebizond was simply ignored by Mehmed, his reply was:

> "Mother, in my hand is the sword of Islam. Without this hardship I should not deserve the name of gazi (warrior of faith), and today and tomorrow I should have to cover my face in shame before Allah!"

When Trebizond's ruler, David Comnenus heard that Sultan Mehmed himself had brought his army to encircle his city from both land and sea, he immediately tried to make peace and save himself. Trebizond was a bejewelled amphitheatre with lush greenery and stunning palaces encrusted with domes and towers, castles and houses. Atop its houses were rich gardens with flowering orchards and vines. In the centre of the city was an acropolis surrounded by fortified walls, trenches and iron gates to taunt and dismay invading armies. Anchored on a cliff, the imperial palace towered above this ancient Greek vista.

The grand vezir sent the following message to the emperor of Trebizond:

> "To the Emperor of Trebizond of the imperial family of the Hellenes, Mehmed the Great King, declares: you see how great a distance I have traveled after deciding to invade your territory. If you now surrender your capital without delay, I shall make over lands to you as I did to Demetrius, the Greek prince of Morea, on whom I bestowed riches, islands, and the beautiful city of Aeros (Enez). He is now living at peace and is happy. But if you do not give ear to these proposals, know that annihilation awaits your city. For I will not leave this spot until I have levelled the walls and ignominiously killed all the inhabitants."

The threat was clear, making the Emperor Comneni more despondent as no ally was willing to send any support. The emperor called for a conditional surrender, which Mehmed was unwilling to accept, but his advisers persuaded him to. The emperor was allowed to take all his treasures with him and left the city to the Janissaries. His people were enslaved, with 800 of their youth enrolled in the Janissaries. Mehmed gave David Comneni a governorship post and an annual income of 300,000 pieces of silver.

The conquest of Sinop and Trebizond during 1461 involved no fighting because the mere presence of Sultan Mehmed led to their surrender. By now he was the sovereign of the northern coast of Asia Minor, which spanned from Eregil to the borders of Armenia. The fall of Trebizond and Sinop further devastated the crusader and Turkoman hopes of defeating the Ottomans.

* * *

Wallachia and Dracul

When Mehmed's father, Sultan Murad II, was alive he had drawn up an agreement with the Wallachians to pay an annual tax for their autonomy. Wallachia was 'The Romanian Land' situated to the west of the Black Sea. Sultan Murad II had given Vlad and his brother refuge in the Ottoman court when their father was killed by John Hunyadi. During Mehmed's reign, this annual tax continued until the Wallachian Prince Vlad III became Voivode, ruler in 1456 and stopped paying. He was confident that he was powerful enough to attack the Ottoman Empire. Mehmed's spies informed him that Vlad had proposed to the Hungarian King Mathias to send an expedition against the Ottomans.

Vlad III was famous for being a brutal and bloodthirsty prince. However, the Hungarians remained in alliance with him just to stir up trouble for Mehmed. Vlad's nickname was Tepes, the Impaler, and Dracul, the Devil. He either impaled thousands of people or cut them into pieces or burned them alive. Once he enjoyed a feast in his court whilst nearby he had a group of Muslims impaled alive. There were countless reports about the terror that he unleashed. He enjoyed torturing prisoners by removing their toenails and having goats lick salt of them. Dracul nailed the turbans of Muslims to their heads, burned the beggars in his city alive; and even opened the belly of his own mistress to see whether she was with a child.

The first attempt by Mehmed to end Vlad's horrific reign was to trick him into coming to Istanbul and have him imprisoned. Vlad was ordered to bring the annual tax with him and 500 Wallachian *diversme*. He agreed but he was cautious enough to bring his bodyguards and was ready for any surprises. En route to Istanbul, the Ottomans led an unsuccessful ambush. Vlad and his troops managed to counter attack and imprison Ottoman troops including Mehmed's commander of the Danube territories, Hamza Pasha, and his Greek secretary, Thomas Catavolenus (his Muslim name was Yunus Bey).

Sultan Mehmed was infuriated with Vlad's reign of terror who had impaled an estimated 25,000 prisoners. Approximately 100,000 to 150,000 soldiers were gathered and 25 triremes and 150 smaller vessels sailed through the Black Sea into the Danube. Mehmed joined his fleet and left Istanbul on 26 April 1462. Tursun Beg said that "whenever the Sultan was present in battle, the outcome was favourable."

It was obvious from his large army that Mehmed's intent was not only to end Vlad's reign but to also subjugate Wallachia as he had done with its neighbours, Greece and Serbia. However, Wallachia was not easy for the Conqueror to defeat. It was made up of scattered villages on the base of mountains with few cities. Upon disembarking into Wallachian territory, the Ottomans burned its port and destroyed much of its countryside. To ensure that his troops remained ready, Mehmed ordered that they were to remain in marching formation. While crossing the Danube, the Ottoman infantry faced no army. This was because Vlad knew that the only way to withstand the might of the Ottomans was to withdraw into the dense oak forests, where all his people and their livestock had sought refuge in.

Mehmed did not meet any challenge across the deserted

Wallachian plains and became more confident when his spies relayed that the Hungarians were not sending any help. Vlad had sent desperate letters to the king of Hungary reminding him that once Wallachia was under Ottoman rule then Hungary would be next but he had only received silence.

Vlad's knowledge of the terrain gave him the edge, enabling him to wage a guerrilla warfare against the Ottomans. He led a surprise attack on one Ottoman camp and tried to find Mehmed's tent, but instead he could only reach the animals. The Ottoman troops pursued his fleeing troops and captured 1,000 prisoners who were immediately executed. These skirmishes showed Vlad how powerless his army was.

Mehmed then turned his attention to capturing Wallachia's capital city, Tirgoviste. His army reached an empty city, its gates open and there was no army to defend it. But a heinous sight confronted Mehmed. He was horrified to see more than 20,000 impaled Bulgarian and Muslim bodies. In the midst of the corpses, he saw Hamza Pasha's impaled body on the tallest stake because of his high rank.

While Vlad tried to engage the Ottomans in small-scale attacks, he was never able to gain the upper hand and instead escaped to Moldavia. He left behind 6,000 troops to continue the fight without him. Approximately 2,000 of these troops were captured and beheaded. In a matter of thirty days the Wallachian army was annihilated and their wealth and land was taken by Mehmed's conquering army. He appointed Mihaloglu Ali Bey as the governor of Wallachia to support and install Vlad's brother, Radu, who was the opposite of Vlad, as the Voivode of Wallachia.

Vlad's escape meant that he had lost all his power and influence in Wallachia. He took refuge in Transylvania. It's believed that from there Vlad tried to send a letter to Mehmed, promising to help him gain power over Transylvania and Hungary. But this letter never reached Sultan Mehmed. However, news of it did reach the ears of King Mathias of Hungary who immediately sent for Vlad and imprisoned him in Buda until 1476. On his release, he was sent to fight the Ottomans. However, Vlad and his small forces were ambushed and he was promptly beheaded with his head sent to Istanbul.

* * *

Lesbos

Returning from Wallachia to Istanbul in victory did not ease or lighten the attitude of Sultan Mehmed. He was now thirty years old. He put serious restrictions on communications leaving Istanbul, particularly by Europeans to their countries of origin. Even smugglers were fearful of carrying any missives. Confiscation of copper, lead and leather goods began to take place. People assumed that a new secretive expedition was being planned or that Mehmed was preparing for an attack.

The Greek island of Lesbos was, however, Mehmed's next target. To pursue this campaign and ensure its success, he gave careful attention to the development of the Ottoman navy. He built a naval base in Istanbul where large warships were housed.

There were many grievances against Lesbos and its ruler, Niccolo Gattilusio, a Genoese who had come to power by strangling his own brother. Mehmed resented that Niccolo allowed Catalan pirates from north-eastern Spain to roam the Anatolian coasts. Gattilusio had given these pirates shelter and shared in their spoils, which also included Muslim slaves. Secretly he was also plotting with the Italians and kept delaying the tributes.

Mehmed with his Janissaries sailed through the Dardanelles to Lesbos. On passing Hisarlik, the legendary city of Troy, he reflected:

"God has reserved for me... the right to avenge this city... It was the Greeks who ravaged this place... now through my efforts, paid the penalty."

Mehmed's naval force included 60 galleys and 125 vessels of different sizes. His fleet carried siege machines, catapults, mortars and around 2,000 stone balls. Mehmed's first plan was to get Niccolo Gattilusio to surrender. He sent him an encouraging letter promising him to keep his possessions if he agreed to reside elsewhere. Niccolo refused, with the belief that his island's fortified castles and troops would resist the attack. His army numbered 5,000, which also included 70 Knights of Rhodes and 110 Catalan pirates.

Mehmed gave the order for six of his largest cannon to batter the walls of the main city of Lesbos, Mytilene. For ten days, the city experienced nothing but intense bombardment. The outer walls collapsed and the inhabitants all took refuge within the city's inner walls. They desperately tried to repair the walls with anything they could scavenge. But there was no hope of rebuilding the outer walls because most of their soldiers were too busy looting the wineries. Mehmed boarded one of his triremes to reconnaissance the walls and find its vulnerable spot. He then ordered a full scale assault. When his Janissaries entered the city, they found most of the defending troops drunk and unable to muster any resistance.

Gattilusio was caught and brought to Sultan Mehmed. At first, he tried to appeal to Mehmed and asked for wealth equal to his heritage. But knowing his appalling position, he ended up falling at the feet of Sultan Mehmed, begging for his mercy. Gattilusio gave all sorts of excuses to explain his actions, blaming his officials for not surrendering or that he always freed the Muslim slaves brought by the pirates or that his dealings with them were only to protect his own people. He ended his pleas with offering his whole island to the Sultan.

Mehmed was not impressed by Gattilusio's excuses and pleas. He admonished him but did draw a treaty to guarantee the safety of him and his people. He left Mahmud Pasha and his Janissaries to deal with the affairs of Lesbos. The nobles from Lesbos were sent to Istanbul, among them the sister of Niccolo, Maria, a beautiful widow who was chosen for Mehmed's harem. The commoners were left within the city walls while the most able were recruited into the Janissaries.

Lesbos gave Mehmed control over the seas all the way to Egypt, Syria, and even Libya. He then ordered an immediate construction of two fortresses on the Asiatic and European shores of the Dardanelles. The European fortress was called *Kilitü'l-Bahreyn* (Key of the Two Seas) and *Kale-i Sultaniye* (Sultan's Castle). These formidable forts blocked access to Istanbul from the Sea of Marmara but also gave him control over connecting Asia and Europe making him the 'Master of the Seas'.

* * *

Bosnia

During March 1463, Mehmed led another secret mission. He held the supreme command over an estimated army of 150,000 soldiers. However, the Bosnian King had already suspected that Mehmed was aiming to conquer his land. He sent a desperate letter to Pope Pius II beseeching his help and emphasising the Mehmed's insatiable thirst for conquest:

> *"The Turks have built several fortresses in my kingdom and are very friendly with the peasants. They promise that every peasant who joins them will be free... If Mehmed only demanded my kingdom... it would be possible to leave my kingdom to its fate and there would be no need for you to disturb the rest of Christendom in my defence. But his insatiable lust for power knows no bounds. After me he will attack Hungary and the Venetian... Italy... He often speaks of Rome and longs to go there... I shall be the first victim. But after me the Hungarians and the Venetians and other people will suffer the same fate."*

Bosnia was a rugged and impassable landscape, which made its people confident in defying Ottoman rule. Mehmed's spies also relayed that the Bosnian court was in alliance with the pope and Hungary. The pope had asked King Mathias of Hungary to support the defence of Bosnia, however, King Mathias was asking in return for large sums of money and a few Bosnian castles. Bosnia itself was facing a great deal of internal strife as some Bosnians had aligned themselves with the Turks.

Before reaching Bosnia, Mehmed sent his ambassador to claim the annual tax that was overdue. Bosnia was rich in gold and silver mines but the King refused to give the tax. The ambassador warned him that dishonouring their treaty would lead to an unpleasant loss. The Bosnian King immediately sent a message to the Venetians warning them that the Sultan was planning to conquer Venetian land. The Venetians did not take his message seriously and refused to come to his aid. The King then sent a message begging Sultan Mehmed for a 15-year truce.

Mehmed approached Bosnia through its northern trade routes with 20,000 cavalry. Like his great-grandfather, Thunderbolt, his troops arrived and captured countless fortresses. Because Mehmed did not want a prolonged siege, he ordered his large cannons to break down the walls and crush their resistance. This was an effective strategy as most Bosnian towns surrendered immediately. Before Mehmed's arrival, his raiders, *akinci*, managed to capture Bobova. Other Bosnian towns surrendered or were flushed out when their water supplies were cut.

The continuous fall of Bosnian towns increased the Bosnian King's anxiety. He was unable to assemble an army so he fled towards Croatia. However, Mehmed sent his grand vezir, Mahmud Pasha, to pursue him and put an end to all hopes of Bosnian sovereignty. The remaining nobles, aware that their King had deserted them, surrendered and begged Sultan Mehmed for mercy. A total of three hundred Bosnian cities and towns surrendered. Mehmed continued his campaign to conquer all of Bosnia and the only roadblock he faced was Herzegovina, where rugged stony terrain and steep cliffs allowed its inhabitants to resist his army.

The news of Bosnia's conquest reached European countries and they were horrified. Venice sent an urgent letter reminding his fellow Christian brethren of the Ottoman scourge:

> "Impelled by his lust and inexorable hatred of the Catholic faith, the bitterest and fiercest enemy of the Christian name, the prince of the Turks, has carried his audacity so far that among the princes of Christendom there is virtually none willing or even daring to oppose his designs... has not hesitated to advance, arrogantly and with arms in readiness ... almost to the gate and entrance of Italy."

Enraged by the constant expansion of Ottoman rule, Venice feared that it might face a direct attack and in July 1463, they declared war.

In 1464, news reached Hungary that Sultan Mehmed had gathered his army for a new campaign. Approximately 30,000 troops with every kind of siege weaponry had been deployed. The Ottomans attacked Jajce, a fortified town in central Bosnia, which put up a fierce resistance and managed to fight off their attackers. On retreat, Mehmed ordered that all the large cannons be thrown into the river to prevent the Hungarians from accessing them. When the Ottomans left, the Hungarians pulled out one cannon, which was 16 feet long.

The loss in 1464 curbed Ottoman expansion into the heart of Hungary, but the defeat in Jajce was also due to Mehmed's growing ill health. He had become so ill causing him for the first time to stay an entire year within his palace. Nevertheless, two other deaths may have given Mehmed some comfort. His archenemy, Ibrahim Bey, the ruler of Karaman, died in the mountains of Anatolia. And just before launching a new crusade, Pope Pius II also met his death. The pity quarrels between Christian kingdoms would have been a happier news. As the European kingdoms continued their quarrels, the

Florentines hoped that the Turks would destroy the Venetians. Between 1464 and 1465, Mehmed realised that his army needed rest and he honoured them with gifts of horses, clothing and money.

* * *

Albania and war with Venice

In 1466, Mehmed's spies spread the rumour that he was leading an army of 30,000 against Belgrade and Hungary. But instead, the plan was to lead a surprise attack on Albania. The Ottoman's long time adversary was Skanderbeg, who they called Ha'in (traitor) as he had left Islam and returned to his Christian roots and led a fierce resistance against them. The Albanians lived in lofty mountains making their conquest difficult. While Sultan Murad II had captured much of Albania, its most important towns had remained independent and during Sultan Mehmed's rule, they refused to pay tributes.

Mehmed's army besieged the city of Krujë in north-central Albania, but Skanderbeg attacked the Ottoman siege positions from behind. Added to this problem was the Ottoman inability to access supplies. Once the Ottoman general, Balaban, was injured by a musket ball to his neck, the army could no longer continue their attack. Mehmed saw little chance of winning and moved on to another town, Durrës. Before retreating, he decided to build a fort in Elbasan, surrounded by steep mountains, it was to control Skanderbeg and his troops. Skanderbeg tried but failed to capture Elbasan.

The conquest of Albania was on Mehmed's path to capturing Venice. Before the 1463 Venetian declaration of war, Mehmed had shown the Venetians much favour, allowing them to mine in Foça for copper and to trade exclusively in soap production. However, during 1463 most of the Venetians merchants escaped and could not find an avenue to increase their wealth within the Ottoman realms. Sultan Mehmed sent the Venetians an offer of peace, but it did not bear fruit as the Venetians remained adamant about reclaiming Morea and Mytilini. It was easy for Mehmed to reject these claims and instead make his own demands. Mehmed told their envoys:

"You have come here to drink fresh water. Your government gave the king of Hungary enormous sums of money and he did nothing."

Mehmed demanded the return of Lemnos and Irma, an island north of the Aegean Sea and an annual tribute. He was using these tactics to see how war-weary the Venetians were and how far they would go to have peace. He told them:

"Prepare better terms, if you want to enjoy peace and make a treaty with me."

Three years after declaring war, the Venetians were desperate for peace, especially as the trade restrictions had made them suffer economically. The Venetians had lost their status and could no longer match the Ottoman power. They hastily organised their fleet with seventy triremes and mercenaries ready for battle. Their ships carried an array of arsenal including cannons and crossbows. They sailed through the Adriatic and on the isthmus of Corinth they hastily built a fort as their base. One of the Venetian sea captains tried to outsmart the Turks: he lead a surprise attack with twenty-five galleys on the islands of Imroz, Thasos and Samothraki. He even attacked Athens but was not successful. Mehmed ordered Mahmud Pasha to attack and push the Venetian fleet into the sea causing them to flee. The Ottomans reclaimed their lost land and only because of the freezing winter their troops could not pursue the Venetians into the heart of their territory.

The situation for the Venetians on land was much worse: any land attacks were fiercely defeated. During the summer of 1466, 2,000 Venetian troops arrived to capture Patras, once a Greek city, but Mehmed sent reinforcements which easily punished the attacking forces. Around 100 troops were made prisoners and 600 were killed. A revenge attack saw more Venetians killed.

At this stage, the only hope that the Venetians had was in Skanderbeg, the Albanian leader. By now, Skanderbeg was an old man aged sixty and he was also very poor. He had reached out to the pope in 1466 for financial help but the pope had refused him.

In 1467, Mehmed decided to launch another campaign to capture Albania. Mehmed's wood cutters cleared the land for his entire army to cross. Using his bowmen, it was easy to draw out the Albanians and capture the lowlands. But it was difficult to bring down the mountain forts. Mehmed's first target was the city of Durrës. The inhabitants all fled to the mountains and guarded the mountain passes. And the Ottomans were unsuccessful in entering Durrës due to the fierce resistance of its soldiers.

The attack on Durrës frightened the Italians as it was considered an easy route for Mehmed to launch attacks on them. Meanwhile, Skanderbeg used this event to call for more help. The Venetians promised him supplies. North of Durrës, Skanderbeg managed to occupy an Ottoman outpost. Its leader was his nephew who had converted to Islam. Skanderbeg personally beheaded him. He also wore the ring of Balaban, the Ottoman governor of Albania, to emphasise that he had killed him too. Mehmed send troops to capture Skanderbeg who fled to the seacoast and the following year, in 1468, he met his death – not through the glories of battle, but from fever. In the upper realms of Albania, he had beseeched his countrymen to seek the support of Venice. However, after his death his chieftains remained in constant disagreement and could not muster the likes of his resistance.

In 1474, Mehmed returned his attention to Albania. He appointed Sulayman Pasha as head of the army to lead 80,000 troops, including 8,000 Janissaries and around 500 camels carried the heavy artillery. The commander and his army arrived at the city of Shköder in northern Albania, and laid siege. Within four days, four large and numerous small cannons were positioned. Sulayman Pasha cut off all supply routes from the Venetians who were waiting along the Albanian coast.

From May until August 1474, the high walls of Shköder managed to withstand the barrage of Ottoman fire. Both the Ottoman soldiers and the besieged were suffering from disease, shortage of water and supplies. Despite Sulayman's attempt to order the troops to blitz the fortification, it resulted in heavy losses on the Ottoman side; an estimated 3,000 to 6,000 soldiers lost their lives.

A rumour that a Venetian army was coming made Sulayman decide to pull out from this siege and Shköder remained undefeated. There was much rejoicing amongst the Venetians but it did not last long as they learned that Mehmed had increased his naval fleet with 300 ships leaving the Dardanelles.

Five years later, Sultan Mehmed did conquer Skanderbeg's city, Shkoder, and managed to reach every corner of Albania. People cried that *"in all Albania we see nothing but Turks"*.

Negroponte

During 1469, European coastal towns faced a barrage of Ottoman raiders, who also entered the interior of Austria creating widespread fear as far as Venice and Rome.

In 1469, a commander of Negroponte, representing Venetian interests, led a massacre across some Ottoman towns and, in particular, devastated the town of Enez. This made Mehmed reject any notion of ever making peace with the Venetians. As a consequence, Mehmed increased the size of his navy. He used Greek sailors and their knowledge to grow his navy so much so that it could carry an army. The Ottoman market ran out of flour for baking biscuits for the sailors. And in Bursa, all charcoal was used to produce gunpowder. The preparation of Mehmed's mighty navy created deep anxiety and stress in the Aegean coastal towns. They took serious measures to defend themselves, such as arming their population, rebuilding and strengthening their forts and digging trenches. In Chios, no one was allowed to leave the island and all ships were locked up.

In his intense preparation to build a navy, it become obvious to all that the next objective of Mehmed's conquest would be Negroponte. This city was a Venetian jewel representing its glory and splendour and considered by some *"four times better than Constantinople."* The Venetians had always known that Negroponte was on Mehmed's agenda, and he no longer cared about keeping his plans a secret.

The Venetians took serious defensive measures but could only launch thirty-five triremes. Instead, they faced "a gigantic forest of ships" that stretched across nine kilometres made up of one hundred Ottoman triremes and countless vessels. The Ottoman navy had reached such a size that the Venetian sea captain, Niccolo da Canale, was told by his seaman that the Ottoman ships had made, *"the sea a forest. To hear this said seems incredible, but to see it is terrible."* Mehmed personally led his land army – approximately 120,000 troops – while his navy was led by Mahmud Pasha, with 70,000 sailors. There were approximately 300 to 450 Ottoman ships and 108 large triremes, whilst the Venetian forces numbered thirty-five galleys and six freight vessels.

In 1470, the Ottoman forces arrived before the shores of Negroponte, which was well-fortified against land and sea attacks. Upon arrival, Sultan Mehmed ordered a bridge to be built, made up of ships connecting the island to the mainland. Mehmed was well aware of the weakness of Negroponte's fortification, which was on its western side.

During this time Nichola da Canale, the Venetian captain, had taken his fleet to the island of Crete for supplies and troops. He had conveniently missed out on the decisive moments of the battle. When he finally reached Negroponte, his only response to the inhabitants' cries to be rid of the bridge of ships was that the entire fleet needed to be assembled to lead an attack.

The fortified walls of Negroponte delayed Mehmed's conquest.

The Ottomans also faced heavy losses but Mehmed was urged by his adviser, Mahmud Pasha, to continue the siege. There were people inside Negroponte who were accused of aiding the Turks by opening the weak areas of the walls. And some were executed for treason. Eventually, Mehmed's army stormed the city through the weakened walls and conquered Negroponte.

Mehmed's success in Negroponte caused utter fear in Morea, the southern Greek peninsula. While in Venice, days of mourning and prayer procession occupied its populace. They put Nichola da Canale on trial for cowardice and deserting the sailors. He was banished into exile. The Venetian distress was clearly expressed in their letters:

> "The glory and prestige of Venice are destroyed ... all Venice is in grip of horror; the inhabitants, half dead with fear, are saying that to give up all their possessions on the mainland would have been a lesser evil."

It was obvious to the Venetians that they could not face their enemy on an equal footing. They had lost all their wealth and status, and the battles had cost them their best leaders. They had spent seven years fighting the Ottomans and had spent 700,000 gold ducats annually (approximately equivalent to 105 million dollars). Victory was out of reach, as one Venetian wrote:

> "All Italy and all Christendom ... are all in the same danger and there is no coast, no region, no place in Italy which, however remote and secluded it may seem, can be considered more secure than any other. This pestilence and this conflagration are spreading continuously..."

* * *

War with Venice

It was not exactly clear what motivated Mehmed to consider sending an envoy to broker peace with Venice in 1471. Maybe it was the debilitating effects of his ill health or maybe he may have realised that if Venice allied itself with his Anatolian enemy, Uzun Hasan, then this would have delayed his conquest of European territory. But this peace treaty was not a humble nor submissive offer, in fact Mehmed demanded that the Venetians meet a number of conditions. These included a handover of several towns, Aegean islands and an annual head tax: approximately 50,000 Venetian gold ducats, which is equivalent to 7.5 million dollars.

The Venetians were, at this stage, quite desperate to have peace with the Ottomans. It was also humiliating as they had lost so much of their former glory and prestige. They were also fearful that even during peace time there was a chance that Mehmed's forces would raid and capture all that remained of Venetian sovereignty. They saw him as the "king of fortune" whose plan was not just European but world domination.

When the Venetian envoys arrived at the Ottoman court, Mehmed did not meet with them. His reason was that he didn't meet directly with "enemy emissaries". Mehmed did not leave it at that – he also made sure that his conditions for peace overwhelmed them and made the envoys leave immediately. Sultan Mehmed then sent his own peace envoy to Venice, which perplexed the Venetians. It may have been to test whether their intent to reach a peace agreement was serious or not. And it soon proved that they remained foes. The Venetians instead turned to Mehmed's long-term nemesis, Uzun Hasan, and sought an alliance.

On 13 February 1472, the Venetians called the daring Sicilian, Antonello, to lead a raid against the fortified Ottoman armoury in Gelibolu. Antonello broke into fifteen warehouses and set them on fire. A swift fire that lasted for ten days burning 100,000 gold ducats worth of weaponry. Antonello tried to escape with his small band of accomplices but he was caught by Ottoman soldiers and brought before Sultan Mehmed. After listening to him and somewhat appreciating his fearless confession and daring attitude, Mehmed then ordered Antonello and his companions to be executed. Unfortunately for the Venetians, this daring venture had little impact upon the Ottoman arsenal as it had been moved up the Bosphorus.

The woes for the Venetians continued when Mehmed's *akincis* (raiders) led incessant attacks on their frontier borders, reaching within the borders of Hungary, as well as coming within sight of Venice. The raiders were approximately 40,000 horsemen. They built an Ottoman fortress within 50 km of Belgrade and became a base for their raids on Croatia and Carniola. Throughout Mehmed's reign, these raids continued without pause. Together with Mehmed's military campaigns, the raids were terrifying to the populace and were methodically organised and grew in number.

During the spring of 1474, another attempt was made to broker peace between the Ottomans and the Venetians. Mehmed's demands were again exorbitant to the Venetians: payment of old debts amounting to 150,000 gold ducats and surrender of all forts taken by Venetians as well as Krujë. The emissary left with a six-month chance to consider the demands. Before his departure, he was shown the mighty Ottoman army and their preparation to launch another campaign. Mehmed was truly a shrewd negotiator because he used these six months as a safety net to ensure that the Venetians would not consider attacking his territory.

The final attempt to reach peace was through Sultan Mehmed's stepmother, Mara, who tried to broker peace. Two Venetian envoys were sent demanding the return of Negroponte, which did not please Mehmed. In turn, Mehmed's request that they give an annual tax of 100,000 ducats outraged the envoys who immediately left Istanbul and quashed all hopes of peace. The Venetians instead eagerly turned to Mehmed's eastern enemy, Uzun Hasan.

Karaman and Eastern Enemies

Since he could remember, Mehmed had to combat the dogged enmity of Turkoman tribes. The Karaman ruler, Ibrahim Bey pursued a ceaseless campaign to cripple Ottoman sovereignty. He pursued all avenues through making alliances with Western powers or other Turkomans. When Mehmed was occupied with the Karaman rebellions, Venice and Hungary would rejoice that it would take Mehmed months to return to his capital and pursue any military campaign against them. After Ibrahim's death in 1464 and the discord that existed among his sons made it impossible for them to pose a serious threat. Although one of his sons, Shir Ahmed, tried to confront and reject Ottoman authority, however, it was easy for Mehmed to quell his fight and rule Karaman territory, making their resistance futile.

The fiercest and most relentless Eastern Turkoman leader was Uzun Hasan. He was a tribal chief, ruling from his capital Tabriz in northwestern modern Iran. He was famous for his title, "Lord of the White Sheep" and was even considered as the King of Persia. Uzun Hasan had secured alliances with the Pope and the Venetians as well as made contact with the Knights of Rhodes. His envoys to Venice brought with them rich gifts to sweeten their alliance. One gift was a hollow bowl, 23 cm in diameter, made entirely of turquoise and surrounded with lavish jewels of varying sizes. In his letters, Uzun Hasan specifically asked his western allies to supply him with strong ammunition to confront the Ottoman arsenal. The treaty with Venice meant that Uzun Hasan would capture the whole of Anatolia and Venice would recapture the coastlines and territories of Morea, Lesbos, and even Istanbul. The Venetians welcomed and encouraged Uzun Hasan's fights as they believed it would make Mehmed more vulnerable in the east and give them an advantage to launch attacks.

By the fall of 1472, Mehmed had heard much about the expanding army and alliances of Uzun Hasan. During September, Uzun Hasan had sent his army to attack and weaken most of the eastern Ottoman borders. He had gathered a force of 100,000 soldiers and another 100,000 was expected to join. Mehmed responded by first delegating Mahmud Pasha, his grand vezir, to mobilise the Ottoman troops and raise the Janissaries' pay, giving them enough reason to fight.

Uzun Hasan escalated this conflict when his troops attacked Amasya, where Mehmed's son, Bayezid was governor. Mehmed ordered all vessels of different sizes to be seized for his army. He further ordered that 1,200,000 ducats (approximately 180 million dollars) from the treasury to be shared among the populace who joined the army.

The confrontation with Uzun Hasan began perilously. As the Ottoman soldiers crossed the Bosphorus into Anatolia, extreme weather devastated them and their supplies. The storm lasted for four days, destroying much of Mehmed's camp and sinking a number of ships in the Black Sea. These ships were vital as they carried necessary food supplies for the soldiers. If the storm had continued, a quarter of the Ottoman army would have been devastated.

The Ottoman army eventually reached Erzincan near the Euphrates river to face off Uzun Hasan's army. Mehmed's army was grouped into five columns. The first three columns were led by Mehmed, his sons, Bayezid and Mustafa, each having 30,000 troops. Mehmed was positioned in the middle surrounded by the other columns. The governor of Rumelia, Hass Murad Pasha, and Mahmud Pasha, led some 60,000 troops making the fourth column. While the last column was led by the governor of Anatolia with 40,000 troops. This meant that approximately 190,000 soldiers were present, 100,000 of which were auxiliary troops. When Uzun Hasan saw the Ottoman army he wailed, *"Woe thunderation, what an Ocean!"* However, he sent a confident letter to the Hungarian King encouraging him to:

> *"Set fire and flame to the European territory of the Ottomans, because with God's help he (Uzun Hasan) was about to achieve victory over*

the sultan and wished the sultan to be attacked from all sides, so that he would never recover from the defeat and his name would be extinguished for all time."

Unfortunately for Uzun Hasan, both the Hungarian king Mathias Corvinus and Emperor Frederick III remained silent observers in this decisive battle against the Ottomans.

Some of the early attacks led by the Ottomans against Uzun Hasan were unsuccessful. In eagerness, Murad Pasha crossed the Euphrates river with his troops but was immediately surrounded and killed by Uzun Hasan's forces. Mehmed became frustrated with his vezir, Mahmud Pasha, and blamed him for this loss. Approximately 12,000 troops had been killed.

In the midst of this battle, Uzun Hasan sent a messenger who demanded the return of a number of cities. The envoy had brought with him a bag of grain to symbolically show Mehmed that his army needed to be as great as the number of grains for him to win. Mehmed sarcastically poured the grain before a flock of chickens who immediately pecked it. He replied to the messenger,

"Tell your master, that as quickly as these chickens have devoured the sack of grain, my Janissaries will deal with his men, who may be skilled at herding goats but not at fighting."

Uzun Hasan's next move was a surprise attack on the Ottoman camp in the mountains of Erzincan. The Ottoman response was nothing less than terrifying and managed to defeat Uzun Hasan. The Ottoman heavy artillery as well as the *akincis* were the winning ingredients in this fight. Only 1,000 Ottoman troops lost their lives and Mehmed's sons showed courageous leadership and launched themselves into the ferocious battle. Both Uzun Hasan's sons met their end and he himself fled the battle with what was left of his army. His camp and its rich spoils was claimed by the Ottomans. Upon the advice of Mahmud Pasha, Mehmed did not pursue the fleeing Uzun Hasan. And he did not hesitate to spare the lives of the scholars and free 40,000 prisoners.

The 1473 Battle of Baskent battered Uzun Hasan and his Venetian allies. Mehmed immediately sent his army to attack and besiege the Albanian town, Scutari, which was a Venetian neighbour. Uzun Hasan was beaten but his hatred of the Ottomans continued. He hoped that an alliance with the Venetians would help him reach his goal. When the Venetians envoy arrived at his court in Tabriz they saw the appalling state of Uzun Hasan. His only son had abandoned his cause and aligned with the Ottomans by marrying the daughter of Bayezid II and was made the governor of Anatolia. Alone and without much hope to end the Ottoman rule, Uzun Hasan died in 1478, aged in his fifties. However, the next biggest casualty, was perhaps Mahmud Pasha. Mehmed dismissed him from his position for his insistent vouching of Turkoman leaders.

Mehmed was well aware that the Ottoman threat to European powers was now more intense after Uzun Hasan's defeat. Pope Sixtus IV made vain efforts to bring together a crusader alliance and defeat Mehmed. His measures were considered too costly and hollow to save Christendom from the imminent power of the Grand Turk.

During this campaign against Uzun Hasan, Mehmed did not forget his Western enemies. He sent a friendly envoy to the Hungarian King seeking a peace treaty and requested that their envoy visit him. By the time the messenger arrived in Istanbul, Mehmed and his forces were in Anatolia. The messenger then followed their trail and upon reaching the camp of Mehmed, he was given splendid gifts of horses, saddles and much hospitality and entertainment in falconry and hunting. He was sent to the city of Sivas in central Anatolia and waited for three months for Sultan Mehmed to arrive. Mehmed finally did arrive, celebrating his victory against the White Sheep. The Hungarian messenger saw this celebration and was given the opportunity to discuss the treaty; he naively demanded two fortresses close to Belgrade. But Mehmed's response was to reject this condition and in turn demanded Hungarian forts.

Mehmed's call for a peaceful treaty with the Hungarians was really a political ploy. He had played with time to avert any likely Hungarian attack on Istanbul or other Ottoman territory during the campaign against Uzun Hasan, a time when the Ottomans were vulnerable. Even though he had made sure that Istanbul was well-secured, its gates were walled and trenches had been dug by 10,000 workers. And heavy chains were brought and used to block the passage of water between Asia and Europe.

* * *

Death of Çelebi Mustafa

Çelebi Mustafa was Mehmed's favourite son, who had proven his courageous and daring military skills in the battle against the White Sheep. After returning from this battle, he was made governor of Karaman but he also found time to continue his favourite pastimes of hunting and falconry. Within days, however, he began to suffer from a severe mysterious illness that lasted for six months. Once Mehmed learned of Mustafa's illness, he sent 30,000 troops as well as his personal physician, Maestro Iacopo.

Çelebi Mustafa's illness had paralysed him, however, he still ordered his troops to capture the fortress of Develü Karahisar. The inhabitants of this fort only agreed to surrender to Çelebi Mustafa directly. On his deathbed, he was brought before the castle to reach a settlement with its ruler. On his way back, Mustafa's condition worsened and he died. His attendants kept the news of his death secret until they reached Konya. They brought his embalmed body before the palace gates where his mother and daughter waited and wailed their deepest sorrow. Messengers were sent to Istanbul to let Mehmed know of his son's tragic death. He could only show his grief by declaring three days of mourning across Istanbul.

Mustafa was buried in Bursa in 1474 and his wife and mother took residence in the palace nearby. His daughter was married to her cousin, Ahmed Çelebi, who was Bayezid's son. Mehmed appointed his third son, Prince Çem, as the governor of Karaman.

***

Black Sea

By 1475, Sultan Mehmed had total control of the Black Sea, making it his lake. By annexing Caffa in Crimea, all economic activity in this region came under his rule. It also ensured that Genoese colonies came under his authority through their tributes. Control over the Black Sea was vital in ensuring the economic growth and construction of Istanbul. The Ottomans were able to access cheap supplies through the northern Black Sea, this included wheat, meat, and salt. The common trade route from Western Europe through the Black Sea was now in Ottoman hands and Genoa and Venice lost its main trade links. This lack of access through the Black Sea was the reason that forced the Genoese to seek the Atlantic route to reach India and Central Asia, which made possible their invasion of America, *the New World*.

By 1475, supporters for a crusade escalated the fear of the Ottomans. Their rumour mill went as far as printing a manuscript which cited an Ottoman battle cry to invade Italy:

"*Lâ ilâha illallâh; Muhammad rasûlullâh, Roma, Roma* (There is no other god but Allah, Muhammad is His Prophet, Rome, Rome)."

The insertion of Rome within this declaration emphasised how eager the Ottomans were in their quest to capture Italy. Within a short space of time Mehmed's army was within miles of Italy. They became 'masters' of the Adriatic and made the situation far worse for the Venetians who now lost all access to the Adriatic Sea.

Meanwhile, Sülayman was ordered to dig deeper into Europe crossing the Danube and into the Wallachian territory. It was difficult for the Ottoman forces to navigate this foreign territory and build a stronghold as it was full of dense dark forests covered in fog. They faced constant attacks from the Moldavians who showered them with arrows and forced the Ottomans to withdraw. In 1473, the prince of Moldavia, Count Stephen, had invaded Wallachia when Mehmed was busy with Uzun Hasan. In 1476, Mehmed came with his army to confront Stephen who used the dense forests to his advantage and tried to ambush the Ottomans. However, Stephen was unsuccessful and fled losing his hold over Wallachia.

In the battle of Războieni, 1476, Mehmed headed the army against the Moldavian prince, Stephan. The only issue that prevented Mehmed from complete victory was not his enemy but hunger. His troops' supplies were destroyed by a heavy storm, which limited his prospects of continuing a successful campaign. They turned back, but only for a mere ten days because news had reached them that the Hungarian army was on the path to attack Smederevo.

King Matthias Corvinus of Hungary took the initiative to launch an attack on Ottoman territory and capture Šabac, in western Serbia. However, he didn't have the siege artillery that would destroy the Ottoman fortifications. Using intrigue instead, his forces pretended to abandon the siege while managing to enter the fort in disguise and defeat the Ottomans. This victory gave them the confidence to besiege and capture other nearby Ottoman towns. The Hungarian King shared the news of his victory with other European leaders. Their response, however, was to give him financial aid but with some funny commentary. The cardinals gave him 93,000 ducats with a letter that questioned his achievement:

> *"But what can hundreds of thousands avail a poor king against the mighty ruler of Asia and good part of Europe?"*

Mehmed's reaction to the loss of Šabac was to personally lead his forces across the frozen Danube and burn down the forts built by King Matthias. He also meted out due punishment to anyone who had deserted Šabac. His return as commander of the army restored the morale of his troops.

* * *

Peace with Venice

Mehmed continued to push into the heart of Europe. He could not give Venice reprieve until he established himself there. In 1477, his soldiers were within sight of Venice.

> *"The enemy is at our gates!" the Venetians cried. "The ax is at the root. Unless divine help comes, the doom of Christiandom is sealed."*

These desperate cries fell on deaf ears as there was no support from their supposed allies and the Venetian wealth and status no longer matched their enemy's.

The Venetians were by now desperate for peace and waited for Sultan Mehmed to take the initiative. They sent emissaries accepting his demands to hand over Lepanto and to return any territory gained by Sultan Mehmed since 1463 – which included the Greek Island of Lemnos in the North of the Aegean Sea, some mountainous regions – as well as arrears of 100,000 gold ducats (equivalent to 15 million dollars). However, when the Venetians accepted these conditions, Mehmed increased his demands with 10,000 ducats annual head tax. The emissaries asked for a two-month timeframe for the Venetian senate to decide.

The Venetian senate accepted Mehmed's additional conditions and sent their emissary back to finalise the peace treaty. Upon reaching Istanbul, he saw that Mehmed and his army were heading towards Albania. Mehmed was dismissive and pointedly rejected their offer because their response was too late and he was too focused

Sultan Mehmed

on capturing Krujë, a city in north-central Albania. Mehmed added that he would be pleased if they made additional concessions, which included handing over three other Albanian towns. The emissary returned to the Venetian senate who decided against these conditions. And Mehmed turned his forces around and attacked the city of Shköder located in north Albania.

On 1478, the Ottomans set their heavy cannons before the besieged city of Shköder – eleven massive cannons in total. After five days of incessant bombing, the walls remained intact and the inhabitants put up a fierce resistance. Mehmed's war council decided that the siege should continue to bring the defendants to their knees and that the presence of a large army and the Sultan was not necessary. After 12 days and facing towers built by Rumelian and Anatolian troops, Shköder surrendered.

Mehmed then headed to Krujë and the sight of his troops spread a state of urgency among its inhabitants. All their men were sent to defend the fort and dig trenches, while the women and children were moved to the coastal cities. The siege of Krujë lasted a year as the inhabitants' desperation left them with no choice but to surrender.

By now the whole of Albania was Ottoman territory and the incursion of Ottoman raiders made the Venetians lose all hope of maintaining any facade of power or supremacy. Finally in 1478, they sent their ambassador with full decision-making to reach a peace treaty with Sultan Mehmed. They were desperate to keep their trade and accepted all of Mehmed's demands.

It was a humiliating peace treaty for the Venetians, however, it also gave them an advantage. They were allowed safe travel and could take their artillery from their towns but were expected to repay the debt of 150,000 gold ducats as well as 10,000 gold ducats tax for easy trade, an economic advantage that the Venetians clearly saw. Mehmed took key towns in Albania and the Aegean Sea and removed their demands over Krujë and Negroponte, and within two months any land occupied by the Venetians was to be returned. The King of Hungary scolded the Venetians for this treaty and clearly feared that the Ottomans would attack Hungary. It was, however, obvious to the European powers that peace with the Ottomans was the only means to increase their political and economic gains.

During the summer of 1479, Ottoman raiders did reach the plains of Hungary. Twelve Ottoman commanders were sent with 43,000 troops to Transylvania, with the prime goal of capturing important gold and silver mines and salt deposits. Alongside their Hungarian supporters, the Transylvanian army launched an assault but could not challenge the Ottoman forces.

Meanwhile, Mehmed's struggle with arthritis continued during 1479, forcing him to stay within his palace in Istanbul. His illness made it difficult for him to walk or ride across his city to meet with his people. His ailments seemed to increase as he also developed an abscess in one leg. During this time, he pursued his hobbies of gardening, designing bow rings, scabbards, knives and belts. His love of gardening, particularly vegetables, was a common sight. In the palace gardens, he especially enjoyed planting cucumbers.

* * *

The Knights of Rhodes

By 1480, Mehmed had secured his empire in both Anatolia and Rumelia. And it was inevitable that the Knights of St. John in Rhodes suspected an imminent Ottoman attack and immediately fortified themselves.

Sultan Mehmed's son, Çelebi Cem, sent an envoy to the island proposing a peace truce if they paid an annual tribute. The envoy's job was really to observe the Knights' battle preparations. However, the islanders suspected Mehmed's intention and tried to get a three-month reprieve to consider the peace proposal. The delay was intended to help more knights to reach the island from Europe and further prepare their army.

Mehmed was not unaware of the Knights' plans and began his

own preparation. His foot soldiers took the route south from his capital to reach the sixty galleys anchored at Gelibolu. An Ottoman squadron was launched from the Dardanelles to the island of Rhodes in 1480. Led by Mesih Pasha, they besieged the Island for eighty-nine days. The Knights were given a chance to convert to Islam, however, they refused.

Mehmed's spies had informed him that Rhodes was easy to capture as its fortifications were no longer strong and its supplies were meagre. A detailed map was drawn up to help guide projectiles from the large cannons. Once Sultan Mehmed's cannons were fired, they devastated the city walls but the defenders were ready to immediately repair them. Another attempt was made to use a temporary bridge between the harbour and the city wall tower. As the Ottoman troops attempted to cross this bridge, the cables that anchored it were loosened by the defenders. The cannons could not create an opening and thousands of soldiers perished. The Ottomans turned to the Jewish area of the citadel but faced a massive catapult that hurled enormous rocks. On these rocks the Knights wrote 'tribute' just to mock the Ottomans. In addition, they hurled sulphur, pitch and other incinerating objects. Within the castle walls, a number of people were accused of treason and were beheaded or tortured into confessing.

During the night, the sound of *"Allahu Akbar"*, God is most Great, intensified the horror facing the besieged, whilst during daylight the cannons deafened the populace. On Friday, at dawn, an order was given to launch a full-scale assault. It is believed that 40,000 soldiers scaled the walls. The casualties reached 9,000 and 15,000 wounded. General Mesih Pasha realised that the siege could not continue and decided to withdraw from Rhodes. But his assault had devastated the Island of Rhodes, causing the death of half of its knights and the destruction of many of its buildings including the Grand Master's palace, numerous churches and its defence walls.

Meanwhile, on the western side of the Ottoman Empire, Mehmed's *akincis* continued their raids into the heart of Europe.

These raiders numbered up to 16,000. They would divide into three groups and simultaneously led surprise attack across different areas.

* * *

Italy

In early summer, 1480, Mehmed ordered his Grand Admiral, Gedik Ahmed Pasha, to lead the Ottoman navy, comprising of 140 vessels (40 galleys, 60 one-masters, 40 freights) and 18,000 soldiers with 700 horses. The first attack was on the fortress of Otranto, a coastal town in southern Italy. The town dwellers tried to resist and refused to surrender, but when heavy cannons were unloaded from the ships, they saw their fate. Gedik Pasha promised them that the weapons would bring their ruin and annihilation, forcing them to surrender. However, it wasn't long that the Ottoman army itself faced problems as their supplies were running low.

The King of Naples sent an army, which turned the tables and besieged the conquerors within Otranto. The commander, Gedik Ahmed Pasha, soon received supplies that would last for three years, and arrogantly he refused to negotiate their surrender. Instead, he demanded the Italian port cities of Brindisi, Lecce and Taranto and emphasised that if his demands were not met then Sultan Mehmed would bring his army of 100,000 troops and 18,000 cavalry to conquer the whole of Italy.

The rumour that Sultan Mehmed was bringing 200,000 soldiers to Italy created a frenzy and caused an uproar among the Western leaders. The Holy See, Naples, Hungary, the dukedoms of Milan and Ferrara and the republics of Genoa and Florence met to decide on a course of action. They commissioned twenty-six galleys and raised sufficient funds to stop Mehmed. Venice, which was in treaty with the Ottomans, refused to support them because its own fifteen-year war against Mehmed was never supported by these kingdoms.

As spring neared, Mehmed's army was prepared for another

expedition. No one knew what the actual target was, whether he was drawn to wresting power from the Mamlukes (the dynasty that ruled significant Islamic territories across Arabia, Egypt and Levant r. 1250-1571) or leading the campaign personally against the Knights of Rhodes or invading Italy.

On 25 April 1481, Mehmed, while leading his army, became severely sick with stomach pains. Maestro Iacopo, his main physician, claimed that the wrong medicine had been given to him by his Persian physician, al-Lari, and could not be reversed. The medication had blocked Mehmed's intestines. By afternoon prayer on 3 May, 1481, aged 49, Sultan Mehmed gave his last breath.

News of Mehmed's death was kept secret from the army until his body was transported back to Istanbul. The grand vezir, Mehmed Pasha, had taken command and ordered all troops to remain on the Anatolian coast and that no ships could reach Istanbul through the Bosphorus. The grand vezir was seeking to enthrone Çelebi Cem rather than Bayezid. However, the news of Mehmed's passing quickly spread and created utter unrest. The soldiers left their positions, boarded boats and scoured into the palace demanding to see their leader. In a state of fury, the grand vezir, Karaman Mehmed Pasha, and Maestro Iacopo were both murdered.

Bayezid had enough supporters within the Ottoman court and army to ensure that he could replace his father. In a matter of days, he arrived in Istanbul with 4,000 horsemen; the new grand vezir, Ishak Pasha, ensured that Bayezid was welcomed by both the population and Janissaries. The rule of succession was never established in the Ottoman court. It was simply believed that the Sultan would be enthroned through the Will of God, the approval of the ulema, the Janissaries, and other officials.

A solemn funeral ceremony was held for Mehmed where thousands of mourners gathered. Bayezid helped carry his father's coffin and buried him in his *türbe* beside his mosque, *Fatih Cami*.

Mariam Seddiq

Painting of Sultan Mehmed by Gentile Bellini in 1480

Chapter 7

MEHMED'S LEGACY

The Great Eagle is dead! La grande aquila è morta!

There is a portrait of Mehmed in the Istanbul Metropolitan Municipality purchased in 2020 from the National Gallery of London. Mehmed commissioned the famed Venetian portraitist, Gentile Bellini, to paint his portraiture. This painting was made five months before Mehmed's death and was only discovered hundreds of years later in 1865 in the hands of a British explorer and collector. It had been largely repainted which means the original likeness to Mehmed may not be precise.

The Italian Niccolo Sagundino (d.1463) described Mehmed as, "well built, of large rather than medium stature, a man who seldom laughed" with a "rather distinguished mien, with frank, open features." In this painting, Bellini tried to show that Mehmed was in his prime: healthy and fit with a serious expression as he gazes into the distance. He appears deep in thought, his eagle-like stare creating a striking impression. Was he contemplating the conquest of Italy? Or was he planning to wrest power from the Mamluks and control the Hijaz, the sacred cities of Makkah and Medina? Yet he had never organised an army against the Mamluks but had only offered to help them in the management of the pilgrimage in Makkah. As a young boy he had declared that he would be the one to conquer Constantinople, a vision that he fulfilled. We will never know what his next plans were because shortly after this painting, Mehmed died.

Images of Mehmed became plentiful in Europe after his death; he was either portrayed through an admiring lens or one of insidious hatred. Pope Pius II had described Mehmed as "a venomous dragon" who was the scourge of Christendom. It took two to three weeks for the Europeans to learn of his passing and there was much rejoicing. Cannons were fired, fireworks set off and bells rung in celebration. Pope Sixtus led a prayer procession thanking God for Mehmed's death. They all agreed that his death put an end to his invasion of Italy. His death removed the Ottoman chances of launching Otranto as a base to conquer Italy.

In European literature, many of the accounts of the Ottoman Empire occur in the context of war and rivalry. As a result, much of the literature that comes from European sources contains disparaging and sensationalised stories about Mehmed. One story claims that he cut a slave's neck to demonstrate the length of a neck. His modern biographers, Franz Babinger (d. 1967) and John Freely (d. 2017), although providing extensive detail regarding Mehmed's life and his achievements also fall into this trap of narrating unsubstantiated claims. They bandwagon the idea that he was a homosexual who was in love with a fifteen-year-old boy. An allegation which emerged four hundred years after Mehmed's death and without any reference. Homosexuality is a serious sin in Islam and this claim would have destroyed Mehmed's reputation and honour within it. The famous Muslim historiographer, Ibn Khaldun (d. 1406) emphasised that the pursuit of history is to seek the truth. His book, *Al-Muqaddimah*, was one of the first detailed study on historiography. In it he encouraged historians to engage in thorough research and sift through the bias to find the truth. A historian is to fact check, compare sources, and never trust blindly the sources but to apply logic in their understanding of events and people of the past.

Franz Babinger was an orientalist whose writing was coloured by colonial attitudes and stereotype of Ottomans. He did not reference his biography of Mehmed and even ignored key sources such as the primary biographies written by Michael Kritovolous (circa d. 1470) and Tursun Beg (circa d. 1491). It was thus easy for him to associate the controversial issue of fratricide with Mehmed, the killing of one's sibling or brother. Mehmed is accused of enshrining fratricide in Ottoman Law. He is quoted: "Whichever of my sons inherits the sultanate, it behooves him to kill his brothers in the interest of world order. Most jurists have approved this; let action be taken accordingly." Islam regards the killing of an innocent person as a serious crime; it is regarded from among the seven sins that dooms one into the hellfire. In the Qur'an, there are explicit verses that condemn murder and killing of innocent individuals. Allah says:

> "And whoever kills a believer intentionally, his recompense is Hell to abide therein, and the Wrath and Curse of Allah are upon him, and a great punishment is prepared for him." (The Qur'an, An-Nisa', 93)

In another verse:

> "...if anyone killed a person not in retaliation of murder, or (and) to spread mischief in the land – it would be as if he killed all mankind, and if anyone saved a life, it would be as if he saved the life of all mankind..." (The Qur'an, al-Maa'idah, 32)

Only in certain cases, after a judge pronounces the guilty verdict, can a person receive capital punishment in Islam, however, forgiveness and peace are encouraged and honoured. In European literature, Mehmed is accused of encouraging fratricide through killing his own brothers. Some claim that when Mehmed was five years old, he killed his oldest brother, while others accuse him of killing his newborn brother when he became a sultan. These stories were written years after his reign and historians disregard them as they are historically unreliable. They are also disputed logically: why would he be threatened by a newborn?

The idea of killing innocent people is clearly admonished in Islam. Muslims understand from Mehmed's statement that he was not encouraging the senseless killing of innocent individuals. He was arguing that when anyone seeks to bring chaos and attempt to destroy the ruling government to gain power, then that government is obliged to fight them, even if that person is the brother of the ruling sultan. This was a struggle that his father, Murad II, faced against his brother-in-law, Ibrahim Bey, who often engaged in rebellions trying to undermine and topple the Ottoman state. Even his grandfather, Mehmed I, after the death of Bayezid I, spent eleven years struggling to quash the fighting among his brothers that had led to a state of interregnum (the government is in chaos and disarray). Mehmed proposed that rebels needed to be stopped even if it led to death. The aim of Mehmed's law was to prevent a civil war, create stability, good governance, and prevent anarchy.

The Ottomans faced many political rivals who sought to topple their power. Their immediate neighbours, the Byzantines, engaged in much espionage and trickery. They lured or even kidnapped young princes using them as their puppet and a rival ruler to the sultan. When Mehmed II died, his son, Prince Cem, met the same fate. He ended up imprisoned in European courts and was moved about like a puppet as the rival heir challenging his brother, Bayezid II, for the sultanate.

It was this atmosphere of political rivalry and trickery that shadow the cause of Mehmed's sudden death. His health problems began at the early age of thirty-two as he became seriously ill with arthritis. Often, his arthritis prevented him from leading expeditions as he could not ride his horse. He was always loyal and determined to join his troops on the front lines and avoided surrendering to his illness. But it was not arthritis that killed him. Modern historians argue that he was poisoned by his enemies. When Mehmed set out on his final campaign, he was not ill. A week into his journey, he developed an intense pain and within two days he died.

The Venetian archives reveal that Venice sought, for twenty-five years, many avenues to poison Mehmed. The assassins included a seaman, a monk, a barber, and even Mehmed's personal physician and financial consultant, Maestro Iacopo, who was Jewish.

Maestro Iacopo and his Jewish brethren were welcomed members of Ottoman society. While Jewish physicians were shunned in Italy by the papal decree who regarded them as a bad influence upon people and society, the Ottomans, however, welcomed them. Iacopo was first appointed as court physician during Sultan Murad's reign and continued in his role during Sultan Mehmed's reign. However, he never lost touch with his Italian sources and often sought medical books to increase his knowledge, particularly in treating Mehmed's ailments. In 1457, the Venetians had gifted him with 64 meters of fine crimson velvet to vouch on their behalf.

However, the nature of this contact became far more sinister when in 1471, Iacopo was approached with the task of poisoning Mehmed. He willingly agreed but for an immediate payment of 10,000 ducats and a later payment of 25,000 upon achieving his objective. He was given more lucrative promises which included 260,000 pieces of gold if the Venetians did not compensate him within a month of murdering Mehmed. He and his family were promised citizenship and exempted from all taxes. The Venetian plot, however, did not bear immediate fruit. Nevertheless, Mehmed's increasing poor health had become more obvious. During 1471, he could not leave his palace and ten years later, Mehmed died. Historians now emphasise that it was through poisoning, but whether it was the work of Maestro Iacopo or another physician is unknown.

Upon Mehmed's death, Tursun Beg (c. 1426-1491) presented Mehmed's biography to Bayezid II, *Tarih-I Abu'l-Fath, History of the Conqueror*. Tursun was part of Mehmed's *divan* with forty years' experience in the Ottoman court. He was a surveyor and secretary, which was a job given to well-known and trustworthy men. His biography of Mehmed is regarded as the most reliable as it he was an eyewitness to the *divan* and included accurate historical detail.

Tursun admired Mehmed's rule through which the Ottoman empire doubled as 18 new provinces were added. He emphasised that Mehmed modelled five leadership virtues that ensured the success of the empire. These included fear of God, wisdom, courage, honesty, and justice. Tursun described how Mehmed's determination and drive in his conquest of Constantinople continued tenaciously in all of his other conquests. While the Janissaries had rebelled only once, Tursun commented that Mehmed's control stemmed from his honesty and courage. He was never afraid to launch himself fearlessly in the fray of battle with his troops, never asking them to do what he wouldn't do and showing them to seize the opportunity. In between expeditions, he would oversee his troops and recognise their valour and military skills with promotions and rich gifts. And his governors never missed out on prestigious awards and accolades.

Tursun clarified in his introduction, that the purpose of his work was to encourage and advise Bayezid on political stability and good governance. Bayezid II (r. 1481-1512) became the eight sultan, however, unlike his father, he was less adventurous and did not dedicate his life to pursuing the route of conquest. He was more reserved and hesitant, but his father's legacy enabled him to govern for thirty-one years. He was often occupied with the threat of his brother, Cem, who sought to dethrone him. And like his father, Bayezid is believed to have been poisoned by his Jewish physician. However, during Bayezid's reign the Ottoman Empire experienced a more peaceful phase that allowed it to further strengthen and develop economically. This allowed Bayezid to invest in handguns for the Janissaries and construct the biggest Ottoman warships that ever sailed, legitimising their power over the Mediterranean Sea.

Bayezid's son, Selim I (1470-1520), however, did follow the path of expansion but towards Persia, Syria and Egypt and gained the honoured title of *Caliphate Uthmaniyya* when the keys of Makkah was presented to him. Mehmed's great-grandson, Sulayman the

Magnificent (1494-1566) revived Mehmed's spirit of conquering Europe. He managed to conquer Hungary where the Ottoman rule lasted for 150 years (1541–1699). His army also besieged Vienna, the heart of Europe in 1529. By the 16th century, the Ottomans were on the verge of conquering the European world. However, the decisive Battle of Lepanto in 1571 switched the tide of history and ended Ottoman expansion. A coalition of Christian powers which included Spain, Venice, Genoese and the Papacy defeated the Ottomans in the Mediterranean.

For 500 years, Mehmed's descendants cemented the Ottoman influence and presence across three continents. The Ottoman Empire or Caliphate Uthmaniyya in the Muslim world, spanned across Greece, the Balkans, North Africa, western Asia, and the Middle East. A cosmopolitan world was created by Mehmed and his descendants rewarding people for their merit and contribution rather than their birth. From the 17th century, however, the Empire began to decline, as it had strayed far from Mehmed's style of leadership and ambition. The Europeans labelled the Ottomans as "the Sick Man of Europe" and waged an incessant campaign to dismantle its power. The end of World War One marked the end of the Ottoman rule, which was dramatically replaced with the Turkish Republic movement in 1922.

The historian Lowell Clucas in 1988 wrote that Mehmed represented the "complete leader" who was not only a military genius but showed exceptional leadership in the areas of politics, science, and economics. Mary Mills Patrick in 1940 went a little further and wrote: "We cannot study the history of Sultan Fatih without feeling that he was much more civilised than the rulers that existed in his time."

Mehmed has remained for the past 570 years a source of inspiration for the Muslim world. He is famous for his conquest of Constantinople and the expansion of Ottoman empire across the Balkans and Anatolia. While he failed to conquer Belgrade (1456), Rhodes (1480) and Italy (1480), nevertheless his conquest stretched from the

Danube to the Euphrates and far exceeded the territory that Bayezid I had conquered. As the Conqueror of Constantinople, his leadership and military tactics placed him at a lofty rank. After the conquest, Mehmed continued to soar above his contemporaries and played a significant and transformative political and social role in Ottoman society. He managed at a very young age to transform Ottoman rule from a state to an empire and is considered as the founding 'father of the Empire'. He was the first to codify the Ottoman legal system, which later sultans depended on. This revolved around taxation and state organisation that addressed officials roles, promotions, salaries, and pensions. In addition, his other decrees addressed legislation regarding mining, circulation of coins, customs and status of varied groups. He managed the economy directly by controlling all cultivate land and water canals particularly for rice cultivation that ensured that the prices remained low for the population. His leadership was unique in that no one could easily sway him, not even the harem, which became influential in the case of later sultans. He created a centralised government that allowed for consultation and discussion but ultimate decision making remained under his authority.

Mehmed was a charismatic and visionary leader as he had his people's deep loyalty and inspired them to sacrifice their lives and livelihoods to expand the Ottoman Empire and establish the Islamic faith. As a visionary leader, he took risks in technological innovation: this was most obvious in the development of new cannons that transformed traditional warfare. In this manner he continued to encourage the pursuit of knowledge by sponsoring and developing the first university in Istanbul. As a philanthropic leader he was famous for establishing hospitals, schools, waterways, mosques and marketplaces across the Empire. While he sought world domination, he remained a tolerant and cultured leader, who is recognised as the founder of the Ottoman Empire.

Muslims are drawn to Sultan Fatih Mehmed's life because they see him as the one who realised the prophecy of Prophet Muhammad. The hadith that foretold the conquest of Constantinople. Since the 1600s on the wall of Hagia Sophia the famous hadith of the conquest hangs, in gold engraving it reads:

> *"Verily, you shall conquer Constantinople. What a wonderful army will that army be, and what a wonderful commander will that conqueror be."*

While Mehmed's genius and unsurpassed leadership has intrigued many particularly as he rose to rule at such a young age, however, some have questioned whether Mehmed did fulfil this prophecy and wondered as to who associated this hadith to him. Moreover, understanding whether this hadith is authentic and the different Islamic scholarly opinions regarding its content has caused much debate. In essence, historical inquiry compels us to find answers and seek the truth. The early Muslim historians such as Ibn Khaldun's call for historical integrity and inquiry was very much influenced by the hadith scholars whose compilation of hadith literature created a culture of finding the truth.

The hadith of the Prophet has a unique place in Islam. While the Quran is the words of God and is the prime source of Islamic law, the hadith is the Prophet's explanation and demonstration of how to live the Qur'an and is viewed as the second source of Islamic law. Because the Prophet's life was a living expression of the Qur'an, the hadith is regarded by Muslims as equal in value and status to the Qur'an. In the following verses of the Qur'an, God commands the Muslims to obey Him and His Prophet and affirms that the Prophet's endorsement (his hadith) is also revelation.

> *"We have revealed unto thee the Remembrance (the Qur'an), that you may explain to mankind that which has been revealed for them." (The Qur'an, Nahl, 44)*

> *"And whatsoever the Messenger gives you, take it. And whatsoever he forbids, abstain from it." (The Qur'an, al-Hashr, 7)*

Hadith is literally defined as 'communication', 'story', or 'conversation'. In the Islamic context, hadith refers to the body of literature or books that contain records of the Prophet's (peace be upon him) deeds, sayings, silent approval, or description of his physical appearance. The preservation of hadith began during the lifetime of the Prophet. He applied various methods to safeguard his hadith, this included repeating his statements to ensure its memorisation; dictating to his scribe; instructing the Muslims to follow his example and reminding them of the severe punishment in the hereafter of falsifying a hadith. The companions continued this tradition by verifying the authenticity of any statements attributed to the Prophet by directly approaching him to verify hadith. The companions also tested each other's hadith recollection and kept written records of hadith. This culture of preserving and checking the hadith continued and became an established science by the end of the first century of Islam.

The science of hadith, referred to as *'Ilm al-Jarh wa al-Ta'dil'* (criticism or praise), focuses on evaluating the *isnad* (chain of narrators) and the *matn* (content of hadith) to invalidate or declare the hadith as reliable. Hadith were graded into two groups: accepted (maqbul) and rejected (mardud). The acceptable hadith was then categorised as either as authentic (sahih) or good (hasan). If the hadith failed a key criteria, it was then rejected and was labelled as weak (da'eef) or fabricated (mawdoo'). A hadith had to meet five key criteria before it received the label of Sahih. This included: 1) Having a continuous chain of narrators, unbroken and linked backed to the Prophet. 2) Every narrator had a moral character. 3) Every narrator was proficient, with good memory and writing. 4) The hadith would be compared with stronger authority and did contradict the narration of other authorities. 5) The hadith would be compared to other hadith to ensure that they were no hidden defects. A hadith would be totally rejected if it failed to meet the moral character grade. However, if it failed on one other point then it would be classified as Hasan (good).

The grading of hadith was a meticulous science. Scholars checked thoroughly the biographies of each narrator. They compared these hadith with verified hadith to double check for confirmation and contradiction. Then they classified the hadith into the set categories. This thorough investigation involved studying the number of hadith narrated by a narrator; examining the number of their narrated hadith that was verified by other scholars; and studying whether the narrators transmitted alone. It was this meticulous investigation for the truth that influenced Muslim historiographers such as Ibn Khaldun in their appreciation of conducting thorough research.

The famous hadith of the conquest of Constantinople has been recorded in Imam Ahmed ibn Hanbal's hadith book, *Musnad* (reference 355/4, hadith number 18565). Its chain of narrators is as follow:

> "Relayed to us by Abdullah Ibn Muhammad ibn Abi-Shaybah, Abdullah Ibn Ahmed said: "I heard from Abdullah Ibn Muhammad Ibn Abi-Shaybah, said: narrated Zayed bin Al-Hubab say: who told me, Al-Waleed Ibn Al-Mughairah Al-Ma'aferi said: Narrated to me by Abdullah bin Bishri Al-Ghanawi Al-Khatha'mi from his father, that he heard the Prophet (peace be upon him) say: "Constantinople will be conquered, its leader will be great and its army will be great."

An alternate narration includes the following chain of narrators:

> "Abu Yasir bin Abi Habba informed us with the isnad of Abdullah bin Ahmad: He said: my father narrated to me: Narrated to us by Abdullah bin Muhammad and I heard it from Abdullah bin Muhammad bin Abi-Shaybah informed us Zayed bin Al-Hubab, narrated to me Al-Waleed bin Al-Mughairah Al-Ma'aferi, narrated to me by Ubaidullah bin Bashir Al-Ghanawi Al-Khatha'mi from his father: "I heard the Prophet (peace be upon him) say: "You will conquer Constantinople, what great leader its leader will be, and what a great army its army will be."

This hadith has been validated by well-known hadith scholars: Ibn Abdulbarr an-Namari (d. 1071), Muhammad az-Zahabi (d. 1348), Nuraddin al-Haythami (d. 1405), Jalaluddin al-Suyuti (d. 1505), and Muhammad al-Munawi (d. 1622). However, the scholars of hadith have debated the status and authenticity of this hadith. Some scholars have graded this hadith as sahih, such as Hakim al-Nisaburi (d. 1014) who argued that it does meet the criteria of sahih as it is a well-known hadith where scholars have regarded the narrators as trustworthy. However, this hadith has not been included in Bukhari and Muslim's Saheeh collection (*al-Jami al-Sahih*), but it has been included by Bukhari in his book, *al-Tarih al-Kabir* (Great History). However, a consensus among other scholars is that this hadith is hasan (good). The issue centres on the narrator, Bashir Al-Ghanawi Al-Khatha'mi or from his son Abdullah or Ubaidullah, who had two names. Although it was common to have two names during those times, however, this discrepency is the reason why it is regarded as hasan. The scholars who have rated this hadith weak include: Imam Al-Albani (d. 1999) and al-Arnauti (d.2016) and their reason is due to the lack of detail regarding Abdullah bin Bashir and his father. A hadith must meet five criteria for it be classified as sahih, which includes having a continuous chain of narrators.

This hadith was first linked to Mehmed by the Ottoman scholar Şerefeddin Mullah Gurani (d. 1488), who wrote in his commentary of the hadith, that it was 'we who conquered this city through the mercy of Allah', and that Allah granted Sultan Mehmed this victory. The hadith that he associated with their conquest included:

"The first army from my Ummah who will attack the city of Caesar is promised forgiveness.' (Bukhari, "Jihad", 93)

And the hadith:

"Constantinople will be conquered, what great leader its leader will be and what a great army its army will be."

Among the hadith scholars there is disagreement as to who this hadith refers to; whether Sultan Fatih Mehmed realised this prophecy or that it is a prophecy that will be fulfilled during the time of Imam Mehdi. Many scholars hold the opinion that this conquest and the attributes of the leader and the army refer to Imam Mehdi, who will emerge at the ends of time and will lead the conquest of Constantinople. Thus, this prophecy is yet to be fulfilled. However, scholars such as Imam Jalaluddin Al-Suyuti indicated that the hadith of the conquest did not refer to the Mahdi's conquest of Constantinople, but rather to a great Muslim leader and his army. Abdullah bin Bashr Al-Ghanawi Al-Khatha'mi was a tabee (the generation that followed the Sahaba, companions of the Prophet) who reported this hadith from his father to the caliph's brother, Maslama bin Abdul-Malik (d. 738), which made Maslama launch his army across the Anatolian plains and besiege the city of Constantinople. If this conquest was in relation to Mahdi at the ends of times, then this tabee would have acknowledged this view.

There are several sahih hadith about the conquest of Constantinople, which emphasise that this conquest would take place before the 'ends of time', the first battle before the appearance of anti-Christ (dajjal) and not through the efforts of Sultan Mehmed II. Especially as these authentic hadith indicate that the conquest of Constantinople will be achieved without bloodshed, however, in 1453 much blood was shed. Some of the sahih hadiths that are attributed to Imam Mehdi include:

> *"Abu Huraira reported Allah's Apostle (may peace be upon him) saying: "You have heard about a city, one side of which is on land and the other is in the sea (Constantinople). They said: Allah's Messenger, yes. Thereupon he said: The Last Hour would not come unless seventy thousand persons from Bani Ishaq would attack it. When they would land there, they will neither fight with weapons nor would shower arrows but would only say: "There is no god but Allah and Allah is the Greatest," and one side of it would fall. Thaur (one of the*

narrators) said: I think that he said: The part by the side of the ocean. Then they would say for the second time: "There is no god but Allah and Allah is the Greatest" and the second side would also fall, and they would say: "There is no god but Allah and Allah is the Greatest," and the gates would be opened for them and they would enter therein and, they would be collecting spoils of war and distributing them amongst themselves when a noise would be heard saying: Verily, Dajjal has come. And thus they would leave everything there and go back." (Sahih Muslim 2920a)

"Anas bin Malik said: "Constantinople will be conquered with the coming of the Hour." (Jami` at-Tirmidhi 2239)

From the time of the Prophet's death and for many centuries after, numerous attempts were made by Muslims to achieve this conquest and fulfil the prophecy. Abdullah bin Amr bin As, a companion of the Prophet, who recorded the sayings of Prophet Muhammad, narrated the following hadith, which highlights that the conquest of Rome was a recurrent idea expressed by the Prophet:

"We would take notes in the presence of the Prophet and record his ahadith [plural of "hadith"]. At one time one of us asked the Prophet, 'Oh Messenger of Allah! Which will be the first to be conquered: Constantinople or Rome?' He replied: 'Heraclius' city, Constantinople, will be conquered." (Musnad, II, 176)

The companions, their successors, and later Muslims were drawn to this conquest and exerted much effort to attain it. The repeated attempts made by Muslims showed their eagerness to fulfil the prophecy and attain the honour that the Prophet had made to the conquerors. Şerefeddin Mullah Gurani believed that Sultan Mehmed fulfilled this prophecy. He noted that 'we were that army that from the blessing of Allah were present in this conquest and achieved this conquest'. A dream that many Muslims and the sahaba (companions of the Prophet) hoped to achieve. While it is argued that the hadith of the conquest is hasan and it may not be in reference to Mehmed's conquest of Constantinople, however, what remains remarkable is that history regards Mehmed as the conqueror of Constantinople who was a great leader with a great army.

The modern reader can gain a vivid image of Mehmed's leadership and army through the eyes of his contemporaries. Leonardo di Chio, who was a Catholic bishop, helps us enter Mehmed's world and witness the 'greatness' that countless historians have attributed to Mehmed and his army. Chio was in awe of Mehmed and his disciplined army, he wrote:

> "Mehmed, the conqueror of the unconquerable city, stands as a force unlike any we have seen. His armies, well-disciplined and numerous, struck fear into all who heard the approach of their drums. No walls could hold against his cannons, which shattered the fortifications as if they were made of clay. The Sultan himself is tireless, with ambitions that reach beyond the East; he has set his eyes upon Europe, and there is little doubt that he intends to extend his dominion to our lands. His power is unmatched, and the world trembles at the thought of his next campaign."
>
> "The Sultan's army is vast beyond imagination, composed of soldiers from every corner of his empire, united under his banner with a discipline unseen in our lands. They march as one, tireless and relentless, as if driven by some divine force. His Janissaries, the finest of all, fight with unmatched skill and courage, obeying their Sultan's every command without question. No fortress can stand before them, for they are equipped with the most terrible machines of war, and their loyalty to Mehmed is as solid as the steel they carry into battle."

Sultans of the Ottoman Empire

Osman I (Osman Gazi) (c.1258-1324) (r.c.1299 - 1324)
Orhan I (Orhan Gazi) The Conqueror of Bursa (1281-1362) (r. 1326 - 1362)
Murad I (Murad Hüdavendigâr) The Conqueror of Adrianople (1326-1389) (r.1362 - 1389)
Bayezid I (Bayezid Yıldırım) Thunderbolt (1354-1403) (r.1389 - 1402)
Mehmed I (Mehmed Çelebi) (1389-1421) (r.1413 - 1421)
Murad II (1404-1451) (r.1421 - 1444) (r. 1446 - 1451)
Mehmed II (Mehmed Fatih) The Conqueror (1432-1481) (r.1444 - 1446) (r.1451 - 1481)
Bayezid II (1447-1512) (r.1481 - 1512)
Selim I (Selim Yavuz) The Grim or The Stern (1470 - 1520) (r.1512 - 1520)
Suleiman I (Suleiman Kanuni) The Magnificent or Suleiman the Lawgiver (1494 - 1566) (r.1520 - 1566)
Selim II (Selim Sari) (1524 - 1574) (r.1566 - 1574)
Murad III (1546 - 1595) (r.1574 - 1595)
Mehmed III (1566 - 1603) (r.1595 - 1603)
Ahmed I (1590 - 1617) (r.1603 - 1617)
Mustafa I (1592 - 1639) (r.1617 - 1618) (r.1622 - 1623)
Osman II (1604 - 1622) (r.1618 - 1622)
Murad IV (1612 - 1640) (r.1623 - 1640)
Ibrahim (1615 - 1648) (r.1640 - 1648)
Mehmed IV (1642 - 1693) (r. 1648 - 1687)
Suleiman II (1642 - 1691) (r.1687 - 1691)
Ahmed II (1643 - 1695) (r.1691 - 1695)
Mustafa II (1664 - 1703) (r. 1695 - 1703)
Ahmed III (1673 - 1736) (r.1703 - 1730)
Mahmud I (1696 - 1754) (r.1730 - 1754)
Osman III (1699 - 1757) (r.1754 - 1757)
Mustafa III (1717 - 1774) (r.1757 - 1774)
Abdulhamid I (1725 - 1789) (r.1774 - 1789)
Selim III (1761 - 1808) (r.1789 - 1807)
Mustafa IV (1779 - 1808) (r.1807 - 1808)
Mahmud II (1785 - 1839) (r. 1808 - 1839)
Abdülmecid I (1823-1861) (r.1839 - 1861)
Abdülaziz (1830 - 1876) (r.1861 - 1876)
Murad V (1840 - 1904) (r.1876)
Abdulhamid II (1842 - 1918) (r.1876 - 1909)

Sultans of the Ottoman Empire

Mehmed V (1844 - 1918) (r. 1909 - 1918)
Mehmed VI (1861 - 1926) (r. 1918 - 1922)

Bibliography

Alkhateeb, Firas. *Lost Islamic History*. London: Hurst and Company, 2014.

Azami, Muhammad Mustafa. *Studies in Hadith Methodology and Literature*. Kuala Lumpur: Islamic Book Trust, 1977.

Babinger, Franz. *Mehmed the Conqueror and His Time*. Translated by Ralph Manheim. New Jersey: Princeton University Press, 1978.

Beg, Tursun. *The History of Mehmed the Conqueror*. Translated by Halil Inalcik and Rhoads Murphey. Minneapolis: Bibliotheca Islamica, 1978.

Enan, M. Abdullah. *Decisive Moments in the History of Islam*. India: Goodword Books, 2001.

Esposito, John, ed. *The Oxford History of Islam*. New York: Oxford University Press, 1999.

Finkel, Caroline. *Osman's Dream: The Story of the Ottoman Empire 1300-1923*. New York: Basic Books, 2005.

Freely, John. *The Grand Turk*. New York: The Overlook Press, 2009.

Goodwin, Jason. *Lord of the Horizons: A History of the Ottoman Empire*. London: Random House, 1998.

Hart, H. Michael. *The 100: A Ranking of the Most Influential Persons in History*. New York: Hart Publishing Co. Inc., 1989.

Inalcik, Halil. *The Ottoman Empire: The Classical Age 1300-1600*. London: Phoenix Press, 1973.

Inalcik, Halil. *An Economic and Social History of the Ottoman Empire (volume 1: 1300-1600)*. Great Britain: Cambridge University Press, 1994.

Inalcik, Halil. "Sultan Mehmed the Conqueror's Istanbul." 2019. https://istanbultarihi.ist/376-sultan-mehmed-the-conquerors-istanbul.

Kritovoulos, *History of Mehmed the Conqueror*. Translated by Charles T. Riggs. New Jersey: Princeton University Press, 1954.

Küçükaşcı, Mustafa Sabri. "The Conquest Hadith and The Muslim Sieges Of Constantinople." 2019. https://istanbultarihi.ist/423-the-conquest-hadith-and-the-muslim-sieges-of-constantinople.

Mihailovic, Konstantin. *Memoirs of a Janissary*. Translated by Benjamin Stolz. Princeton: Markus Wiener Publishers, 1975.

Najeebabadi, Akbar Shah. *The History of Islam: volume 1-3*. Riyadh: Darussalam, 2000.

Nicolle, David. *The Janissaries*. Oxford: Osprey Publishing, 1995.

Nicolle, David. *The Ottomans: Empire of Faith*. Victoria: Thalamus Publishing, 2008.

Nicolle, David. *Armies of the Ottoman Turks: 1300-1774*. Oxford: Osprey Publishing, 2012.

Bibliography

Said, Edward W. *Orientalism: Western Conceptions of the Orient.* London: Penguin Books, 1978.

Zarabozo, Jamaal al-Din M. *The Authority and Importance of the Sunnah*, Denver: Al-Basheer Company, 2000.

Index

A
Abbasid caliphate, 2, 8, 10
Aegean, 25, 34, 36, 88-89, 93, 97, 112-113, 117, 125, 127
akinci, 17
Albania, 23, 113-116, 128-129
Anatolia, 8, 10, 12, 13, 103,
azap, 17

B
Bayezid I, 14-15, 32, 138
Bayezid II, 124, 133, 140
beyliks, 10, 13
Bosnia, 13, 15, 110-112
Bursa, 12, 22
Byzantine, 4, 5-14, 23, 32, 33, 38, 40-51, 52-67, 136

C
caliphate, 2, 4, 5, 6-8, 11, 141
Constantinople, 3, 5-8, 13-14, 15, 23, 27, 41, 45-67, 140
Crusade, 14, 31-32, 89, 100-102, 115, 124

D
devşirme, 15-16

E
Eastern Roman Empire, (see Byzantine), 3, 5-6,
Edrine, 21
Ertugrul, 10-12

F
Fatih Cami, 76-79

G
gazi, 10-11, 12, 18-19,
Golden Horn, 56-60, 73, 79
Greece, 14, 15, 34-35, 98-100,

Index

H
hadith, 3-4, 27, 45, 55, 67-70, 76, 77, 82, 143-149
Hagia Sophia, (also Ayasofya), 64-68, 73
Hungary, 14, 25, 31, 51-52, 89, 93-96, 108, 111, 120, 124-125, 129-130, 130, 138

I
Italy, 5, 14, 87, 108, 115, 118, 132-133

J
Janissaries, 15-17, 32-33, 41, 63, 94, 99, 122
John Hunyadi, 31, 35, 38, 40, 51, 94, 95

K
Kapıkulu, 17
Kayi, 11-12
khaleefah, 4

M
Mahmud Pasha, 72, 73, 82, 83, 89, 99, 110, 114, 117, 122-124
masjid, 10, 23, 64, 73, 76-77
medrese, 10, 23, 27, 28, 73, 76-77
Mullah Gurani, 27, 59, 61, 146, 149
Murad II, 14, 19, 21, 22-29, 31-39

N
Negroponte, 99-100, 116-118, 129

O
Oğuz, 2, 8, 11
Osman, 11-12, 19
Ottoman Empire, 11-15, 22, 69, 83, 141-142

P
Prophet Muhammad, 2-7, 18, 27, 45, 48, 55, 75, 78, 82, 143-148

Q
Qur'an, 3, 4, 12, 27, 70, 77, 78, 137, 143-144

R
Rightly Guided Caliphs, 4

www.ingramcontent.com/pod-product-compliance
Lightning Source LLC
Chambersburg PA
CBRC090836010526
44107CB00050B/1633